RECIPE TO EMPOWER YOUR LIFE

A WOMAN'S GUIDEBOOK TO SELF-EMPOWERMENT

DR. TAMARA PELOSI

ᴠOOᴋS

CONTENTS

PART II

I dedicate this book to my mother Susan Semerade for standing by me and allowing me the dignity to walk my own path, for not judging me when I judged myself, and for loving me until I could love myself.

Love you, Mom!

PRAISE FOR DR. TAMARA PELOSI

Dr. Tamara Pelosi shares so much of her wisdom in this guidebook, taking difficult situations in her life and turning them into something positive. Her pure honesty in the first part of the book should really give others hope and inspiration.

The second part is packed full of tools (or ingredients) that can be a survival guide to empower others to make positive changes in their lives. I believe through sharing her own experiences others will begin to see the glimmer of light in their darkness.

Dr. Carol Carter, CEO/Family Prevention Professional
Co-founder of Sunshine Alternative Education and Prevention Center

---

I have known Dr. Tamara Pelosi, both professionally and personally, for many years, we met when I served on the board of the Sunshine Center that she co-founded. I recall how Tamara held her head up high never letting the difficult circumstances she was experiencing stand in the way for the children in her care. *Recipe to Empower Your Life* is a testimony not only to how strong a woman Tamara is, but for all women. Her *recipes* for lightening a wounded soul and coming out happy on the other side are some of the best ideas I have ever heard. This book is a must read for all women to help guide them to peace, understanding and success.

Julie Hernandez, Life Coach, Author, Founder of Perspectives Counseling Service and Retired CASAC working over 40 years in the field of addictions and trauma

This courageous, honest and ultimately hopeful memoir and self-help book will inspire anyone who reads it! It serves as a powerful reminder that faith, when mixed with other key ingredients, has the power to heal lives. What a blessing for Dr. Tamara Pelosi to vulnerably share her story of how the *lemons* in her life paved the way for her to formulate this comprehensive recipe. She will indeed impact so many women on their journey seeking hope and freedom.

Dr. Nicole Chiuchiolo, Psychologist and Adjunct Professor, St Joseph's College.

INTRODUCTION

"The first step in the acquisition of wisdom is silence, the second is listening,
the third memory, the fourth practice, the fifth teaching others."
~ Solomon Ibn Gabirol

Fifteen years ago, I self-published my memoir *Pennies from an Angel, Innocent Lives Behind a Crime.* I wanted to tell my side of the story, *the innocent lives behind the crime,* of what my family endured when my husband was convicted of a highly publicized brutal murder.

The events that changed my life forever began on October 21, 2001, on my youngest son Tony's eleventh birthday. On this ill-fated day, my husband Danny Pelosi became the primary suspect in the murder of Theodore Ammon, three years later he was found guilty and sentenced to twenty-five years to life. When the bludgeoned body of the wealthy financier was found in his East Hampton country estate, my life and the lives of my children were never the same again. The death of the New York millionaire instantly became a sensational news story that led to hundreds of stories printed in every Long

Island newspaper as well as lengthy articles in *Time Magazine*, *Star*, and other tabloids. The East Hampton murder didn't stop with the printed word, national TV jumped in with specials on *Paula Zahn Live*, *Primetime*, *Dateline*, *48 Hours*, *Court TV*, and a Lifetime television movie *Murder in the Hamptons*.

I had done the necessary book tours and signings, radio interviews, lectures, and workshops to promote the book. And just like that, I stopped it all. I was done talking about it. I didn't want to keep focusing on such a dark time in my life, which might have been a healthy decision. But the truth is I was still holding onto the shame. I didn't want to rehash that dreadful time in my life. Even though writing the book pushed me to confront some life-long patterns of behavior that were the cause for remaining in a dysfunctional, chaotic, and demeaning marriage and forced me to get out the shovel and dig through the muck and mire to find myself, I also knew a great healing had taken place. But I was still hesitant to share how I found the courage and strength to pick myself up, I incorrectly believed I needed to wait until I had all the answers and not make any more mistakes. Of course, life isn't about not making mistakes. If we never made any mistakes we'd never grow or heal, we wouldn't learn how to cope or evolve and we would never know the meaning of transformation.

Well, the years have sped by. It is now 2020, my three children are adults with their own families. I have four beautiful grandchildren. The baby that I spoke about in the book, my half-sister Seline, is now 15. These past years have been filled with many difficult days and many losses. My sons spent their teen years without a father, I lost a job I loved, my house was foreclosed, my car repossessed, my nineteen-year-old niece died in a tragic car accident. And yet, through the immense heartache, I created my own business "Polaris Coaching and Consulting." In addition, I also work for a private consulting agency, QS2 Inc. I coach Early Childhood teachers and present workshops on Child Development. I created a fourteen-hour course on how to deal with young children's challenging behaviors, and I facilitate women's groups. I also wrote a book, "Recipe for a Peaceful Classroom." I love what I have manifested. And of course, there were other wonderful times as well, especially my daughter's wedding and the birth of my grandchildren.

You're not going to finish this book and be cured. But it's a starting point. One sentence at a time. One page at a time. Change doesn't happen in a week, a month, or even a year. Some days you'll leap forward with great insight, other days you'll take several steps back. But you're collecting your ingredients, and you're cultivating your own unique recipe. And that is how it will go. I am not a person that dwells in the past. When one door closes, it's closed. But I am a person who is willing to learn from her experiences.

What did I do to help me smile again? Well, it took some amazing and powerful ingredients such as two huge bowls of courage, five cups of faith, four cups of self-love, three cups of gratitude, five scoops of positive thinking... all kidding aside, it was these very ingredients that saved my life.

For you to comprehend how powerful this book can be for you I need to tell you what led me from the depths of shame and despair to the insight that enabled me to embrace my life and to be empowered. For only through knowing some of the painful and humiliating circumstances of my past will you understand the "Recipe to Empower Your Life." Many years ago, my pastor told me that God was going to use my experience in a way I could never imagine, "Where I was broken," my pastor said, "the light will shine through." Often God's calling isn't in your plans and it doesn't come when you are living in a blissful state. No, it usually comes from a place of deep pain and the slow process of healing. My experience will be someone else's survival guide. I know people are waiting, and most of all it's okay not to be perfect because I am perfectly imperfect. So here it is – I am taking the plunge and bringing my story to the surface again.

There is no doubt this book can help you. I am the living proof.

PART I

1982-1990

A WEDDING, A HONEYMOON, BABIES & CHAOS

"Life is a succession of lessons which must be lived to be understood."
~ Ralph Waldo Emerson

The insanity began on the first day of spring, March 21, 1982, my wedding day. It rained like a monsoon. I was eighteen, pregnant, and floating somewhere around cloud nine. I can't say the same for my mother. Her feet were firmly planted on the ground. She wasn't keen on this relationship from the start. Everyone who knew Danny Pelosi, including my mother, warned me from the beginning to stay away from him. I was told he was bad news and that he was bound to break my heart. But it was too late. I was madly in love. When you're young and innocent you live in the day, not in the future. Dan told me to trust him and I did. He said he would never hurt me. I believed him. Visions of a white picket fence and happily ever after danced in my mind. I never got the white picket fence and the happily ever after part lasted for as long as it took to plan our simple old-fashioned Italian-American wedding. Danny strolled into the church nearly half an hour late sporting a stupid grin on his face, his tie askew, and his hair and tuxedo wet from the rain. He cracked jokes about having one last beer as a single guy. My parents were upset, but I didn't care. He showed up and we were going to be married. Danny was waiting for me at the altar. His tie was straightened. He was joking with the best man who jabbed him in his arm and Danny poked him back. The bridal party chuckled. But the stone-faced pastor didn't find it very amusing. In a stern voice, he pronounced us husband and wife. Husband? Wife? Us? We looked at each other and broke up, even we knew we looked more like teenagers dressed for the prom. In spite of the fact that Danny dawdled on his way to the church, it was a wonderful wedding. I could not have been happier. Our family helped in decorating the local yacht club with white crepe streamers with clusters of white balloons tied along the bridal table. The long buffet tables were filled with delicious homemade foods cooked by my relatives. There was enough food to feed an army of guests with hearty appetites. The liquor flowed, the music played, we danced to the Tarantella, crooned along with the old-timers and mashed wedding cake in each other's face to the roar of our friends. This was by no stretch of the imagination a high-priced gala event. It was families gathered in affection and support who toasted us a long life of love, health and happiness. Dan's father told us we had a long rocky road ahead of us, and said if we loved, honored and respected one another we had a chance. Maybe we would have had a chance had we loved, honored and respected not just each other, but ourselves as well. Statistically, we were doomed from the start, two young teens with about as much maturity as a preadolescent. The torrential downpour on the day of my wedding was surely an omen of what lay ahead.

We set out for our honeymoon, two foolish kids in a souped-up 1968 red Camaro headed for the Poconos. We drove most of the way with the bottom of my wedding gown sticking out the door. I never thought to change clothes to something more appropriate. When we stopped for gas, I needed to use the ladies' room and stepped out of the car into a huge puddle. The entire bottom of my gown was soaked. We drove the rest of the way to our honeymoon resort with me in my muddy wedding gown and Danny in his stained wrinkled tuxedo. We arrived at the resort in our rumpled attire holding hands and giggling like the two kids we were, so young in fact that we couldn't toast our marriage with a glass of champagne. We didn't care. We were in love. We had life in the palms of our hands.

My parents built us a cozy little apartment in their basement. For a short while, we liked playing house. I did a little cooking, every so often I threw some clothes in the washing machine, (my mother's machine), and swept the floor. Dan bought us some used furniture, hung a few pictures on the wall and went off to work with my father. It was sort of fun. My daughter Rachelle was born some months later. Neither Dan nor I knew much about raising babies. What we did know was that we loved her. To prove his love, Dan had our names tattooed on his arm. A symbol of our love and unity. I was on top of the world. I had Danny, a baby and a little place of our own, even if it didn't have a picket fence.

Neither Danny nor I behaved as adults. Whenever we got into a squabble, which was often, I'd run upstairs to my mother's and complain to her just as I had done when I was a twelve-year-old snitching on my younger brother. For a while, my mother played the role of mediator. Eventually, she tired of our childish bickering and in no uncertain terms told us it was about time we acted like a married couple.

It wasn't long after my daughter's birth before Danny got bored with his new role as husband and father. Having a baby didn't stop him from partying. He began going out on Friday nights and stumbling in as the sun was coming up. Friday nights progressed to Saturdays. Sundays he stayed passed out in bed. The following weekend it would start all over again. I'd scream at him like some old fishmonger, but he'd ignore me and walk out the door. I became preoccupied with his whereabouts. In the middle of the night, I'd bundle my infant daughter and drive around town looking for Dan in the local bars. I was obsessed with finding him. When I did, I'd storm into the bar cause a ridiculous scene and make a fool of myself. In the end, all it did was keep him out longer. Some people told me Danny just needed time to sow his oats. I gave him a long time. I gave him the majority of my life.

There was always some event or episode with Danny, from barroom fights to scrabbles with the police. Around 1985 he had his first thirty-day stint in rehab. I believed he would come home cured. He didn't. He proceeded to pick up where he left off. Nothing changed. Danny drank. Danny partied. I held steadfast to my foolhardy illusion that one day we would be that happy little family I fantasized about.

The insanity continued for years. Of course, while living in the madness, it simply became a part of my everyday life. I never recognized the progression of dysfunction. There was no definitive line down the middle letting me know what was normal and what was not normal or what was acceptable and what was not acceptable. It just was.

There was nothing unusual about Dan's staying out until the wee hours of the morning. In fact, it had gotten to the point that I preferred when he wasn't home, then I could concentrate on my studies. When I was pregnant with my daughter, I had gone back to college part-time working on my Associate's Degree in Early Childhood Education, which

Danny thought was a waste of my time. He constantly belittled me and told me I would never amount to anything.

Our marital squabbles turned into feuds and feuds manifested into raging battles. On one of the many occasions Danny stumbled in the door in the early morning hours and passed out on the couch, I knew the best thing for me to do was stay in bed and hope for some sleep. I fought back the rage welling inside me but to no avail. The stench of alcohol sent me over the edge. I charged out of the bedroom like a crazy woman. Danny was sprawled out on the couch, his mouth wide open like a dead fish, saliva drooling down his chin. In blind fury, I slapped him hard across his face. From his drunken stupor, he pulled me down on the floor. I spat in his face and kicked him in the groin. He scrambled up, grabbed his shoes, stormed out the door, and squealed out of the driveway. I had completely lost control of my emotions. I had turned into a lunatic. My three-year-old daughter was crouched in the corner of her bed. She wrapped her skinny self around my body like a baby monkey and tucked her small head under my chin. This discerning toddler patted me on the back and told me not to cry. By the time Danny got home that night, I had scrubbed the apartment squeaky clean, made him his favorite meal and had my hair done. I believed if I kept a cleaner house, cooked better meals, and looked prettier, Danny would change. He didn't. I tried another strategy; I bought a sexy purple nightgown. That caught his attention. Danny decided we needed another child, a boy. He assured me things would be different if we had a boy. The sexy nightgown didn't keep Danny home, but it did get me pregnant. By this time, I was down to ninety pounds from one hundred fifteen, rather scrawny on a five-foot-four-inch frame. I avoided looking at myself in full-length mirrors. I was a walking skeleton. I prayed for a boy.

Surprisingly, Dan settled down. He willingly turned his paycheck over to me which allowed us to catch up on some bills, with some money left over for a night at the movies. For the first time in three years, Danny cared for his daughter while I was at school. He even bought me a new typewriter as a token of his support for my academic efforts. Our lives were on a smooth and even keel. I stopped waiting for the other shoe to drop. I shouldn't have.

My life was akin to an avalanche. First, there are those little warnings, a few small rocks that tumble down, then a huge boulder pitches down the mountainside and crashes into my naïve unsuspecting nature. There was a boulder heading in my direction for several weeks, but I chose to ignore it, certain it would change direction. But boulders of that magnitude do not change their course; rather they build in speed and momentum. First Danny's late for dinner, then he's not home for dinner, half a paycheck, then no paycheck, gone for an hour, gone for the night. The signs were so obvious but I was in too much denial to see them, or rather, believe them. I was told that the cigarette butt I found in the ashtray of Dan's car was from his friend who borrowed the car the week before and what appeared to be a smudge of red lipstick on his shirt was from a red pen. The best was the blatantly unmistakable hickey on his neck and Dan's incredible explanation that it was a bruise from a piece of lumber that scraped against his neck when he was unloading it from the truck. He had an answer for everything. When I confronted him with the rumor I heard, that he had been seen with my girlfriend's younger sister, he said that was ridiculous and I shouldn't believe trouble makers,

One week before my baby was born, I was hit square in the heart from that runaway mammoth boulder. I was on my way to a class and something made me take a different route, one that was slightly out of the way. I had this horrible feeling in the pit of my stomach. I knew I was about to come face to face with my worst fear. I turned down a side street and saw Danny's car in the driveway of my girlfriend's sister's home. I drove up and down the road a few times not knowing what to do. I parked the car, walked boldly to the front door and found it unlocked. Like a burglar, I tiptoed in, marched down the hallway and discovered the two of them in all their glory. Temporary insanity, that's what I called it. Blame it on my hormones gone wild. I attacked with my bare hands, slapping and hitting anything within range. Danny ran off abandoning me in one of the worst situations of my life. Much of what happened is a blur. I made it home, but I don't know how. I do remember standing in front of the bathroom mirror and the shock of seeing my face. I looked aged and haggard, my eyes sunken and dull. It wasn't the face of a twenty-three-year-old woman happily awaiting the birth of her child. I spotted Danny's prescription painkillers that he had from a back injury. I opened the bottle and counted twenty-three pills. I rolled the smooth little pills around in my hand. For one fraction of a second, one millisecond, I contemplated the thought. *I could end it all here and now. He'd come home and find me dead. Then he would know how much pain he had caused me.* I dumped them in the toilet.

I dragged my swollen aching body to the couch. I was emotionally drained, numb. I was mortified by my behavior, my lunacy and what I might have done to my unborn baby. I wanted Danny to come home and beg me for forgiveness, to beg like a dog so I could tell him to get out. I wanted him to suffer and be in pain. I fell asleep on the couch hugging Rachelle's Winnie the Pooh pillow in my arms.

Dan came home some hours later with his head hanging low in that forlorn way. He knelt down on his knees just the way I wanted him to. He covered his face with his hands and sobbed like a baby. I'm ashamed to say I didn't say a word. Instead, I told him everything would be okay. He didn't have to beg me for forgiveness. With the unspoken word, I had already forgiven him.

One week later I went into labor. After four grueling hours an almost nine-pound baby boy, Little Dan, entered the world in the winter of February 1986. Danny said a boy would complete our family. I caressed my newborn son's velvety cheek. I had great expectations this sleepy baby boy would alter the course of his father's life.

Several months later there was no indication that Danny was going to make good on his promise. Having a son didn't change his behavior any more than having a daughter did.

The routine of our lives stayed the same. I returned to school and completed my Associates's Degree with no further encouragement from Danny. The electric typewriter he had bought me as a token of his support had been flung across the room in a heated dispute. On countless occasions, I considered professional help, but there always seemed to be sufficient reprieve to take a breath and trust that Danny would have that turnaround I so desperately prayed for. Life continued to be one giant-sized roller coaster of mixed emotions. As many times as Danny made me cry, he made me laugh. As often as I hated him, I believed it would work. As much as I wanted him to leave, I prayed he'd never leave. I saw the good in him and closed my eyes to everything else.

A few days after Little Dan's first birthday my mother came into the kitchen holding some Al-Anon literature in her hands that one of the girls at her job gave her. I scanned them suspiciously. I didn't need to read through each one to know that was where I needed to go.

My mother came with me to my first meeting. I was terrified. There were a small group of women sitting around a long rectangular table; each one shared their own personal story. Gratefully no one asked me to speak.

During the coffee break, the group milled about and laughed among themselves.

I marveled at the gaiety and lightheartedness of these people who had just revealed painful experiences.

The pretty young woman who had sat at the head of the table introduced herself to me. She didn't ask me any personal questions but spoke briefly about her home life. She told me her name was Carol and said if I kept coming back my life would change as hers had. At the close of the meeting, each of the women came up to me and gave me a genuine hug. They told me to keep coming back. And I did.

Even though my home life remained chaotic, I found peace and serenity in my heart and kept coming to meetings to refill my empty cup with awareness, acceptance and love. I discovered a faith I never had and trusted that Danny would get help when Danny was ready, in Danny's time and in God's time. It didn't mean I loved him any less, it just meant I was learning to love myself.

It was months before Danny found out I was going to Al-Anon meetings; he wasn't happy, but I continued to go anyway. The people I met there were kind and understanding. Instead of dragging my children along to search the bars for their father, I brought them with me to my meetings. Each time I went I learned something new. It was a long time before I had the courage to share some tidbit of my life, but I listened intently and soaked in what I heard. One of the most profound things I learned was I did not cause Danny to drink, I could not cure him and I had no control of his drinking.

What a relief that was to discover it was not because I didn't keep a sparkling clean house or a meal was overcooked or I happened to say the wrong thing at the wrong time.

I am grateful I had Al-Anon when Danny was arrested for driving while intoxicated. A thirty-day sentence was mandatory in the state of New York. It was believed by most people, primarily myself, that Danny's time at the county jail, and not at a rehab, would knock some sense into his hard head. He'd come out a new man, or at least come out a man and own up to his responsibilities. It worked – for a while. Dan got a good job as an apprentice electrician. We were able to save enough money to move out of my parent's home and rent a lovely house with a great view of the bay. We even got a couple of dogs to complete the almost perfect picture. It wasn't exactly heaven, though Dan had stopped drinking, *again*, and the bills were paid, *again*. But he still was out at night until the wee hours of the morning. The way I looked at it, at least he wasn't drinking and we didn't fight as much.

On Mother's Day, he bought me flowers, not just a bouquet of roses as most men would do, but over thirty flats of annuals and perennials. Dan did do things in a grand style. It's not the unusual abundance of flowers that stands out in my mind as much as the memory of us planting the flowers together.

It was a magnificent garden, but it was only a façade. While the outside portrayed cheerfulness and light-heartedness, inside my heart I was despondent and hopeless. I often cried myself to sleep, lonely, confused, aching for Danny to be home with me. On one such lonely night, I had been in a deep sleep when I was startled awake by a bright light shining in my bedroom window. I slid out of bed and crawled over to the side window and peeked behind the curtains. I saw some cars in front of the house and men in suits. The dogs began barking and running through the house. Their racket woke up my son. Crouching down, believing I was under some sort of an attack, I scurried to my son's crib and soothed him with his bottle.

There was a pounding on the front door. I threw a robe on and opened the door a crack, but one of the men pushed the door wider. He told me his name, Detective something or other, and flashed a badge in my face. He asked me where Danny was and if I was alone. He warned me I would be in big trouble if I withheld information on Danny's whereabouts. The whole time he questioned me his dark eyes peered around the room. He made lewd remarks about Danny leaving such a pretty wife by herself. I was nauseated with fear. I didn't know if these men were really detectives or not. They continued to intimidate and interrogate me; finally, they left. I locked the door and shut off the inside lights and stood hiding behind the curtains. I waited there until I heard them drive away. My heart was beating so loud I felt it pulsating in my ears. From the corner of my eye, I saw the back door creak open. I lost my breath - it was Danny. He was crawling in on all fours like a Marine in combat; his clothes were drenched and stunk of canal water. He writhed his way around and managed to pull down the attic ladder, grabbed a towel then stole his way up the rickety stairs as light and nimble as a monkey sailing up a tree, leaving a trail of water behind him. He told me to stay quiet. Danny stayed in the attic all night. I hid under my covers trembling. When he finally did come down it was almost daylight and his clothes were still damp. He made up an elaborate story about his truck breaking down and swimming across the canal rather than walking the distance to get home. I knew this wasn't the truth. I never found out what actually happened that night or who these men really were. They never returned and I chose not to pursue it. Danny would only lie further. The event was dropped, never discussed and life resumed.

Six months later Danny was arrested again for driving while intoxicated; his second DWI. This time he was away for four months at a prison farm for rehabilitation. We almost made it one full year living in the little house. But without an income, I had to move back to my parent's and leave my home with the beautiful view of the bay and the enchanted garden behind. The kids were too young to understand why I was crying. Every box I hauled out to the car brought an onslaught of fresh tears. When my two-year-old son asked in his squeaky baby voice if we were going to take everything, even his bedroom walls, I lost it. How could I tell my little child that the walls are going to stay, and the house and garden and the beautiful view of the bay, that the only things we were taking were some measly possessions because it would be crowded living in my mother's home? Of course, I said nothing. Instead, I had the kids pick a bouquet of flowers from the garden to bring to their grandmother. We piled in the car and headed to my mother's. From the rearview mirror, I took one last look at the little house with the view of the bay and the Montauk Daisies in full bloom dancing around in the breeze. Living at my parents was as arduous as I imagined it would be. Not because of anything or anyone in particular. It's simply difficult to have two families live together under one roof, especially when there are small active children.

My mother sent the kids and me to relatives in Florida for a month for some R & R. She hoped being away in the warmth of the southern sun would be healing. She pleaded with me not to have any contact with Danny; I heeded her advice. I was rested by the time I returned. Having no communication with Danny for an entire month, undoubtedly had something to do with feeling renewed. However, there was a stack of letters from him piled on my bureau when I returned home.

I wonder if things would have turned out differently had my mother thrown away his letters. But she didn't. Danny wrote a letter every day. His letters demonstrated the daily progression of his recovery process. He had taken responsibility for his actions and behaviors and began to make amends to the people he had hurt. The words he spoke on paper were mature and sincere and not full of the line of bull from the past. I was confident Danny had reached his bottom and was prepared to turn his life around. I counted the days until he would be home. The past was the past. We both were committed to the task of accepting our mistakes and moving forward.

Danny came home on Memorial weekend of 1989. When I saw him after four long months, I fell in love again.

We moved out of my mother's home and rented a lovely three-bedroom house that I found while Dan was away. We spent the day moving furniture and hauling boxes. That evening after the kids were bathed and put to bed, Dan and I collapsed on our deck squeezing together on one chaise lounge. Some events in our lives remain in our minds and hearts forever, every detail so vivid you can recall the faintest smells and the slightest sounds; the fishy odor of the fertilizer newly dug in the field across the way, the silence of the night interrupted by the hum of a low flying plane, even the whiff of Dan's aftershave floating in the air. He was wearing jeans and a white tee shirt with his pack of Marlboros rolled up in his left sleeve. Dan had pulled me close and wrapped his arm around my shoulder. I could hear the gentle rhythmic beat of his heart. I had everything I dreamed of. That evening as we snuggled in bed together, we talked about our future. We hoped we had learned by our past errors, mine as well as his. We accepted we would live each day one at a time. I had no regrets. I was proud I stuck it out and I was proud of him. As two mature adults, we made a conscious, sober decision to have another child. I felt secure and loved. The kids, too, were thrilled to have their father around, particularly Little Dan. He followed his father around like a puppy at his heels. Wherever Big Dan was, Little Dan was two steps behind. He wore little work boots and had his own tool belt, hammer and all, just like his dad. On the evening of the fourth of July, we saw a spectacular firework show. Little Dan was perched on top of his father's shoulders, his pudgy hands wrapped in Danny's. Above the deafening booms of the fireworks, my little son said, "I so happy Daddy's here waters coming out my eyes." I think that profound statement out of the mouth of a three-year-old just about summed it up.

A year later Dan remained sober. He was ambitious and motivated and started his own electrical business. He bought a good used truck, new tools and equipment; the phone rang with customers looking for an electrician. We saved enough money and purchased the home we had been renting. Throughout this time, I plugged away at school moving forward with my Bachelor's in Education. Danny took care of the kids when I had night classes. We came a long way from the days I hunted the local bars for him. What a difference sobriety made. About six months later I found out I was pregnant with our third child. It was a unique and gratifying experience to plan a child as two stable and responsible adults.

Our third child, Anthony, nick-named Tony from the start, made his grand debut on a cool fall day in 1990. A few months after our son Tony was born, Dan added a second tattoo with his sons' names in two banners above an American eagle. This was Danny's way of sealing in his commitment to his family, his badge of protection and guardianship. We were a happy family for quite a while. One day, in particular, stands out in my mind as if it were yesterday. A snowstorm that howled in during the night had created drifts over four feet high. In the morning the view in my backyard looked like a Hallmark card. The evergreens were draped in thick white wraps; the sun sparkled off the pristine snow. Danny had the kids out right after breakfast. I stayed in baking chocolate chip cookies. I wiped the steam off the window and peered out at them having fun. Danny was like the Pied Piper trudging through the snow with the kids and dogs following in his tracks. They were covered from head to toe in the soft white powder. For hours they frolicked outside in the giant-sized igloo Danny built. All four of them crawled inside the icy dome, even our overweight Dachshund. I could hear their muffled giggles from inside the house. Hot cocoa and warm cookies were ready for them when they came in. It couldn't have been more perfect than that.

The best years of my marriage were the years of sobriety. It was during those years I had everything I could possibly want, a sober husband, healthy children, a beautiful home and dear friends to share in my joy. No one can take these memories from me. They cannot be deleted and sent to the recycle bin as if they never existed. They are mine to cherish regardless of the fact that I probably clung to them longer than I should .

THINK THE UNTHINKABLE AND DO THE IMPOSSIBLE

"We cannot tell what may happen to us in the strange medley of life.
But we can decide what happens in us—how we can take it, what we do
with it—and that is what really counts in the end."
~ Joseph Fort Newton

In 1991 Carol and I attended an inspirational three-day nationally recognized drug and alcohol prevention program for children. The workshop was presented by a beautiful spiritual woman named Patti, who immediately became our dear friend. The program utilized colorful hand-sized puppets to teach children the necessary skills to cope with life's challenges. Because the disease of alcoholism affected both our families, we hoped to find a way for our children to break the cycle of addiction and guide them into a healthy alcohol and drug-free future. We needed $400 to purchase the programs' kit in order for us to get started. We began with a yard sale that, even though it poured like the dickens, we raised exactly the amount of money that we needed - $400.93! Our mission was underway. We carted our mobile puppet program to libraries, community centers, scout meetings and any other place that would have us. Before long we progressed from visiting facilities to renting some space in a church basement where we could offer more programs for youths and their families. For years Carol and I worked without pay. Our reward was the hugs from parents of young suicidal teens who turned their lives around. Our good work spread rapidly throughout the community. The more we offered, the more calls we received. The demand for our programs progressed at an overwhelming rate which meant we outgrew our limited space in the church basement. We needed a more permanent structure to expand our ever-growing programs. We realized the importance for us to plan for the additional funding that was needed and managed to collect enough resources to take care of the legal matters. Then we enlisted officers of our new organization. Since I was the one in charge of collecting the money from the workshops (a whole ten dollars that I carried around in a paper bag), I was elected the treasurer. Carol had taken on the responsibility of writing letters and designing flyers, so she was nominated secretary, and Patti who helped us through the entire process and was our main source of financial backing was elected president. Carol, Patti and I had tremendous faith; we not only believed in miracles, we expected them, and trusted that God would continue to lead us where we needed to be. After some extensive research and many prayers, the town granted us an abandoned dilapidated farmhouse on sixteen acres of private wooded land, all for the price of $1 per year. Our prayers were answered above and beyond our wildest dreams. There was a catch though; the rooms were gutted, wires hung from the ceilings, rotting musty smelling insulation was piled in heaps and there was a nauseating stench of a decayed dead cat. But it was ours. We spent weeks making calls for assistance and received a tremendous outpouring of help. Hundreds of volunteers from plumbers and carpenters to retired citizens and teens donated their time, energy and resources. Carol, Patti and I created a place of recognition within the community. Over the years the center's walls were covered with plaques and proclamations from the town honoring our services and scores of pictures of the three of us shaking hands with the town's politicians. We were a success in every way, except one, our resources. We never knew where the next dollar was coming from. Like my personal life, we ran in the red for years. We were working over forty hours a week and wearing a dozen different hats, but we were never able to raise enough money for us to draw a decent salary. It was frustrating to all of us, but Carol and Patti had their husbands to depend on. I on the other hand had to listen to Danny tell me to *get a job that pays*. We depended on miracles to support us, but the center was sinking financially. Patti, never one to give up on her faith, was sure we would pull through, and of course, we did. One autumn day an attractive woman with a recent degree in marketing approached our center. By the end of the afternoon, Diane signed on as our personal financial consultant, pro bono. As a shrewd businesswoman, Diane taught us how to make the most use of what little money we had and how to make that money work for us. In a matter of months, she had our sorry affairs underway and we were able to draw a decent salary. Within a few years, our center evolved to a quarter-million-dollar business that offered a variety of educational workshops and support groups, including a successful summer program and preschool.

1993-1999

LIES, LIES AND MORE LIES

"Truthful lips endure forever, but a lying tongue lasts only a moment."
~ Proverbes 12:19

It was around 1993 when Danny had been doing some electrical work on one of the homes in the new development not far from our home. He became friendly with the owners, a couple around our age, and wanted me to meet them. Dan made the arrangements for the four of us to get together for dinner. Beth and I immediately hit it off and quickly became good friends.

It was during my friendship with Beth when Dan and I began the slow but steady tumble from the peak to the valley far below. Dan became distant, he'd jump down my throat if I asked him a simple question. I was concerned Dan had started drinking again, although there was no evidence confirming that. He was angry about everything. He never talked, just argued or gave me the silent treatment. For several weeks this odd behavior continued. I could not approach him on any matter. I avoided him as much as possible and buried myself in my work. When he moved himself out of the bedroom and took up residence on the living room couch, I confided in Beth. She suggested the possibility that there might be problems with Dan's business. She said her husband always acted weird when a customer was giving him a hard time. This made perfect sense to me.

One morning while Dan was in the shower, his beeper went off. Normally I would ignore it figuring it was probably one of his workers. But some little voice told me to pick it up. In bold letters, the message read – "THINKING OF YOU!"

Thinking of you? Thinking of you!

At last, the pieces of the puzzle fit. Of course, that was it. He was having an affair.

I didn't wait for Dan to get out of the shower; I barged in, threw the curtain back, ripped the hooks right off the shower rod and shoved the beeper in his face. He was quick with an answer, never raised his voice, just said it was probably the wrong number. He grabbed his beeper from my trembling hand, stepped around me as if I had some dreadful oozing skin disease, got himself dressed, and out the door he went, muttering over his shoulder that I was nuts. With a quivering hand, I dialed Beth and told her about the mysterious beeper message and my suspicions that Danny was screwing around. She assured me it had to have been a wrong number; Danny wouldn't have been stupid enough to give out his beeper number. I tried to convince myself that this was the truth, but there were too many unanswered questions and things that didn't make any sense. Danny seemed to know about things I hadn't told him, like the time Beth and I planned on attending our boys' preschool play. I had a commitment at work that I couldn't get out of so Beth went without me. I had no intention of telling Danny I didn't go. But the next day he criticized me for being an unfit mother and going to my ridiculous job that I didn't get paid for. He also knew about a credit card that I had received and hid in my daughter's bureau drawer. I was sure he had the phone tapped. But couldn't imagine why. The next time I spoke with Beth on the phone I asked her to go for a walk with me. I told her my suspicions of the phone being tapped which would certainly indicate that Danny was having an affair and he was checking to see what I knew. Beth seemed concerned too. We both agreed we shouldn't talk on the phone anymore. I had never told Beth about Danny's affair he had when I was pregnant with my second child and thought this was as good a time as any. Beth was speechless. She had a hard time digesting this information. In fact, she seemed extremely upset.

I wasn't able to stop my mind from spinning, haunted by the need to find some shred of evidence that Danny was cheating. But aside from Dan's abrupt change of attitude, I had nothing to go by, no lipstick smears, no mysterious bruise on his neck, nothing, nada, zilch. Nevertheless, I was obsessed with proving I wasn't going off the deep end. I even asked a friend to check if the phone line was tapped. It wasn't. If the phone wasn't tapped, I couldn't imagine how Danny had access to information.

With Danny sleeping on the couch and our marriage steadily falling apart, I thought it best if he moved out. At first, I thought about putting his things in his truck while he was sleeping and then locking the door when he left in the morning, but I realized that wouldn't work. He'd have a fit and I'd be the one putting his clothes back. I considered writing him a letter. I knew that wouldn't have worked either. I would still have to face him. If I wanted him out, I would have to be bold and tell him to his face. But the timing never seemed right and months went slipping by. It was an odd arrangement with him on the couch, but I adjusted to it. At least I didn't have to confront him. In the meantime, Beth and I continued with our friendship.

Out of the blue or it seemed like out of the blue, Danny came home one night and told me *he* was leaving. Not exactly leaving because he couldn't afford to actually move out and rent someplace, he'd move into the garage apartment that he had built for my mother some years before when she finally found her inner strength to divorce my father. I didn't think Danny's idea was a bad arrangement. He would be out of my sight, more or less. I wouldn't have to see him, cook for him, do his laundry or listen to his lies. In my demented mind, I could still keep tabs on him. I would know when he was out, what time he came home and I could catch him with someone else. It became my nightly routine before going to bed to look out the window and check if Danny's car was in the driveway. If it was, I could fall asleep, if it wasn't, I'd jump out of bed every time I heard a car. Crazy thoughts would race in my head. I'd imagine myself going into the apartment and finding him with someone else just as I had years before. Eventually, I'd fall asleep from sheer exhaustion. This was how I allowed myself to live. I fell into the mundane routine of Dan in the apartment and me in the house and went about my everyday life. Sometimes he would eat dinner with the kids and me, other times I wouldn't see him for days. Every opportunity I had I'd spy in the apartment when I knew he wasn't going to be home in the hopes of finding something. I never let go of my insurmountable need to learn what I believed was the truth.

There were some advantages to not having Danny under my roof, I had the bathroom to myself in the morning, and I didn't have to jump out of bed first thing and make his coffee, I could even watch whatever I wanted on TV. Not much, I admit. He still controlled the finances and I still needed to grovel like a low-ranking dog for a chunk of meat. I had to continue to play the game as I always did - by his rules. I'd ask him for money. He'd ask me for what. I'd tell him the bills. He'd tell me he's getting a check. The same old script. The bills were due and I needed money. This was always a great excuse for me to go to the apartment and see what he was doing. Sometimes I'd listen at his door before knocking in the hopes of catching him doing something. This evening Danny seemed to be a little too cheery and a little too willing to give me money without me having to go through the customary groveling routine. He was in the middle of writing me out a check and announced in a matter-of-fact way, as if he was telling me he bought new tires for the car, that he had been seeing this girl, Mary, he met one night while he was out. I ignored him, figuring he was just saying this to get a rise out of me and waited for him to give me the check. But he was telling me the truth or the truth as Danny knew it. He told me Mary was a nice person and I'd like her when I got to meet her. I stormed out of the apartment, and decided to call Beth even though it was nine-thirty and I knew her husband didn't like it when she got calls in the evening. I begged her to take a ride with me and used the excuse that we forgot to pick up some supplies for the kids' art project. When I told Beth Danny had finally confessed to his affair including the woman's name and all the details, Beth went ballistic. A few days later Danny actually had the audacity to bring Mary to the apartment. I watched her trot along behind him. His new puppy. I was frothing at the mouth, furious beyond words that he would actually bring this woman on my property. But I placed all the blame on Mary. How dare *she* violate me; how dare *she* step foot on my property. Had I given it any thought I would have realized that this woman probably didn't know what was going on. She might have believed that Danny was renting a studio in someone's house. I never admitted to Danny just how angry I was, but at least I was brave enough to tell him I didn't want his girlfriend on my property again.

Some women may believe I should have insisted that Danny leave completely, not just let him live in his convenient little hide-a-way. But others may relate to my inability to act. As absurd as this living arrangement was, I felt like I had some connection to him. Somewhere deep down I still foolishly believed we could make our marriage work.

The week between Christmas and New Year of 1997, I went to the movies and saw the romantic yet tearful, *Titanic*, with my daughter. I noticed Danny's car wasn't in the driveway when we got home but heard him a few minutes later. My fifteen-year-old daughter and I were both feeling weepy and downhearted from the sad movie and plopped ourselves down on the couch with a box of tissues when Danny called me on the phone and asked me to come over to the apartment; he had something he wanted to talk to me about. My stomach went queasy; I didn't like the tone in his voice. I stepped into the apartment and found Danny sitting on the chair with a newly lit cigarette in his hand. I caught a whiff of sulfur from the match. He pointed to the chair across from him for me to sit. I sat. I didn't like the pinched look on his face or the tightness in his jaw. Danny took a long drag on his Marlboro. He let the smoke come out slowly, tapping his cheek to create smoke rings. Growing impatient I asked him what he wanted. About half a dozen things raced through my mind in less than a fraction of a second. None of them good. Dan hesitated for a moment, blew out one or two more smoke rings then while clearing his throat told me he had been seeing my dear friend Beth. I didn't believe him. He was sicker than I ever imagined. In the middle of my screaming at Danny, calling him a liar and accusing him of trying to ruin my friendship with Beth, my daughter came over to the apartment. I totally ignored her and continued shrieking. I never noticed she was crying. I screamed at Dan, who screamed back at me, my daughter screamed at the both of us. She was trying to tell us that her brother had thrown a fork at her arm and she was bleeding. The entire household had gone crazy.

The boys had been off the wall since Danny moved into the apartment; they were either having yelling matches or worse, punching each other. I would usually hide in the basement doing my best to ignore the chaos around me. My teenage daughter became the peacemaker and caretaker. I refused to listen to any more of Danny's story. I stormed out of his apartment, called Beth and told her I was on my way to her house without explaining why. I sped to Beth's like a fireman called to a burning building, not even slowing down for the stop sign. I screeched into her driveway and blasted the horn. I have no idea what Beth told her husband, but she raced to the car in her slippers throwing her coat over her pajamas as she ran. We sat for over an hour in the 7-11 parking lot sipping coffee trying to figure out why Danny would have made up such a horrible lie. *He* was the liar. *She* was my friend. *He* was the low-life slime. I believed her. Danny was gone by the time I got home. He didn't come home that night. I didn't see him until the following night when he again called me and asked me to come over. He was standing at his door waiting for me. I pushed my way past him not knowing what ridiculous story would come out of his mouth. What I heard that night was more painful than anything I could imagine. He told me he was going to prove that he had been seeing Beth, he also added, they had been having an affair for three years. Dan dialed Beth's phone number; at the time it didn't register in my brain that he knew her number by heart. Dan clicked the phone on speaker and put his finger to his lips, signaling me to stay quiet. He told Beth he had confessed to me. Her voice over the receiver was loud and clear. She wanted to know why Danny would tell me when they had already agreed that I shouldn't find out. Their relationship was over, and according to Beth what I didn't know wouldn't hurt me.

I might as well have been shot with a high-powered rifle, the pain was that severe; I felt as if my guts had been blown out of my body, splattered all about me. I stumbled out of the apartment and ran to the house, tripped on the back step and fell forward scraping my knees and hands. I ran through the house like a madwoman for the phone and snatched it away from my daughter who had been innocently chatting with a friend. Her bubbly teenage light-heartedness instantly switched to fear. I dialed Beth's number in record speed, she had little to say. She never meant to hurt me. In between her blubbering sobs, she pleaded for me to forgive her. She didn't intend to fall in love with Danny, he was a great friend, it kept getting deeper and deeper, she knew it had to end. Blah. Blah. Blah. I hung up before she could say anything more and collapsed in a heap on the kitchen floor. My young daughter bundled me up in her young arms and comforted me as if I was the child, just as she did when she was a two-year-old. With my head on her bony shoulder, we cried.

Danny remained living in the apartment and continued his fling with Mary. I *never* spoke with Beth again. But I did find out why Danny *confessed* to me. It had nothing to do with his guilt. Nothing to do with his morals. And nothing to do with Danny not wanting to hurt me. Ironically, Beth ended their wanton affair when she discovered Danny was seeing Mary. Apparently, Beth couldn't deal with the fact that Danny was cheating on *her*. And so, to hurt Beth for breaking up with him, Danny confessed to *me*. So, while Danny was cheating on *me* with *Beth*, he was cheating on *Beth* with *Mary!* They don't make soap operas this sordid!

Not more than a few weeks after my life was torn to shreds, Danny informed me that he and Mary rented a place and were taking up residence somewhere else. Dan might have been out of the house, but he was not out of my life. Suddenly he became the good father and he *and* Mary would come over on Saturday mornings and take *my* sons to play baseball. Mary went out of her way to be pleasant with me. She seemed sincere and enjoyed having my boys with her and they liked her, which I had a difficult time accepting. I reasoned that the boys were young, only eleven and seven years old, and needed their father. I was thankful that my daughter had no interest in being a part of the newly formed family.

I should have been grateful that Danny moved out, but I wasn't. I had a hard time coping with the fact that Danny actually left me. And even a harder time admitting that whatever Danny was looking for, he couldn't find with me. Interesting to note the females that Danny sought were women who were going through their own hell. These women had low self-esteem, they were weak and ready for someone to take away their pain. I fit into their category.

As it turned out, Danny and Mary only lived together for a few months. In June of 1998, Dan went to jail for his third DWI. I had heard Mary visited Danny in jail, but after a short while, she cut all ties with him. Bravo, for Mary, she at least had some sense to get out before it was too late for her. I took advantage of Danny locked behind bars and initiated divorce proceedings. But Dan refused to sign the papers. I suppose without Mary around Danny remembered he had a wife. Instead of him signing the papers he began to write me long letters, just as he had done in the past. He poured out his heart, his shame and his remorse. It didn't take long for him to snare me again. He was a desperate man at this point and I was making threats I had never made before. Dan reached deep into his bag of tricks and set his bait in a steel heart trap.

It worked. I was tricked like the starved fox tempted by a morsel of meat who gets itself caught in a steel leg device. I grasped onto that morsel of meat and ignored my raw and bleeding heart.

In January of 1999, after spending six months in jail, Danny was back at home. I had done a superb job of placing Danny's affairs and every disappointment in a neatly stacked mental folder that I labeled - "Don't Open – EVER." I knew everyone thought I had gone completely crazy taking him back again. But I thoroughly convinced myself that Danny finally came to the point in his life when he was ready to take responsibility for his actions and reached the threshold of maturity. I was certain he had come to his senses; after all, he had plenty of time in jail to reflect on his life. I prayed so hard for him I forgot to pray for myself. I was totally incapable of seeing my own delusions and illusions and crazed way of thinking. I didn't need Danny's line of bull to sucker me in. I was fully capable of duping myself. My ridiculous dream of husband, family and white picket fence, thrust its delusional head up like a persistent crocus pushing its way through the snow-crusted surface. We were in a financial mess, worse than we had ever been in. We had already filed bankruptcy a few years before and had two mortgage payments because of it. I was working but my income could not cover all the expenses. Danny had sold his work truck and many of his tools before going to jail to help pay for his attorney. Without ample cash, Dan couldn't return to his own electrical business. Eventually, he found some odd jobs, enough to keep ourselves above water and put food on the table. Danny was confident that we'd be back on our feet in no time. I wasn't anywhere near as positive and stuffed my fears deep enough to ignore. The initial excitement I had felt when Danny came home faded rapidly. I had put on a good front and pretended so well that I actually fooled myself into believing him. I was grateful he wasn't drinking; we weren't fighting and he was home to take the burden off my shoulders of raising three kids alone. In time Danny's persistence and confidence landed him a good job as an electrician on the eastern end of Long Island. For almost two years we lived as most ordinary couples. It was good long enough to fool me.

I had foolishly stopped going to Al-Anon. I knew the steps that I needed to and didn't take. It had gotten to the point that I was too ashamed to talk to anyone. I thought I'd try counseling, but it didn't work for me at the time. I was no more willing to talk to a stranger than I was with the familiar group at Al-Anon.

For the short time that I did try counseling I was at least honest about my childhood because, in my perception, it wasn't bad. In fact, I thought we were a happy family. My parents were still married while most of my friends came from divorced homes. I didn't have a bad relationship with my father, I simply didn't have one. He was the absentee father, a workaholic turned gambler turned alcoholic. He was the type of man who exploded if the bread wasn't fresh or if dinner wasn't to his liking, any ridiculous thing could set him off; it all depended on whether or not he had a good day at the track. He was a man of few words with an unobtainable dream, particularly to retire at a young age as a wealthy racehorse owner. He followed his dream until it eventually swallowed him whole and us along with him.

I grew up on a small horse farm, including not only the racehorses but a few goats, sheep, a couple of pigs and a menagerie of dogs and cats. It was my father's fantasy to have a barn full of expensive and prized racehorses. But it was my mother that did all the work on the farm, from mucking stalls to grooming horses, tending to the small livestock and maintaining a large farmhouse to boot. My father was one for starting things and not finishing them. A carpenter and mason by trade, and an intelligent and talented man, he could erect a building from an image in his mind, but could not complete the work on our house. We lived at the farm for years in a house that was partially finished. The downstairs bathroom never had a sink installed, the slate floor in the kitchen was incomplete, water pipes to the barn were never dug. If my mother wasn't happy, she did a good job of concealing it, especially from us kids. I never knew her to complain. Unlike my father who went into rages, my mother rarely raised her voice, except with my younger brother who could even get a saint to lose its temper.

My memories of living on the farm were happy ones. I had my own horse and had won several ribbons at the 4-H Club events, I watched in amazement as our mare give birth, I fed baby pigs a bottle, I skated on the small pond in the backfield that froze over in the winters, and I ate ripe apples off our trees. It wasn't a bad life for a child. In my senior year we moved to a smaller house closer to town and within walking distance to school and all of my friends; a move that I didn't find distressing. It wasn't until I was an adult that I learned my parents lost the farm due to my father's gambling. I wasn't aware how my mother suffered silently at the loss of the home she loved dearly and the animals that she cared for, some from birth that had to be sold or given away. My mother being the master of cover-up never revealed her sorrow; instead, she did her best to make our new house into a home, even though this house as well, remained unfinished. For a while my father stopped gambling long enough to accumulate some money, he renovated the house and installed an in-ground pool, but par for the course, once the gambling resumed whatever was not finished, stayed unfinished.

That was the basis of my childhood, a father who wasn't around much, a mother who hid her feelings; parents who didn't argue, but didn't communicate, happy holidays with relatives, but no family vacations, a mother who tried to do it all, a father who never noticed, a brother who acted out and me who stayed in the background. Not exactly *Father Knows Best*, but not horrendous either.

After three months of delving into my childhood and avoiding the real issues of my life, I stopped going to counseling and steadily progressed within my own disease; from living in the insanity to being the insanity, to being in denial, to being numb. One day rolled into another, day turned to night and night came back to day. The sun came up. The sun went down. That was the one consistent thing in my life. I plunged into my education and received my Master's Degree. In fact, I had been working on my thesis when I was doled the crushing news about Beth and Danny.

Every day, regardless of what was going on around me, I went to work. I'd shower, put on make-up, and dress like the professional I was – at work. No one knew my guts were held together by a sheer Band-Aid, one wrong move and they'd spill out. Work was my refuge, my sanctuary, a place for me to hide. There I was looked upon as having it all together, a competent, confident, intelligent and sane woman. I could forget about myself and reach out to others. It was my job and the center that Carol and I founded that kept me alive; it was my therapy. As long as I had my work, I was functional, or so it appeared.

2 0 0 0 - 2 0 0 2

FROM RAGS TO RICHES

"Whoever trusts in his riches will fall,
but the righteous will thrive like a green leaf."
~ Proverbs 28:20

In the early spring of 2000, Danny came home from work excited about meeting with an old friend of his. The friend told him about a job that he was working on in New York City, renovating a huge apartment building for an extremely wealthy woman, Generosa Ammon. He also mentioned that the woman was in the middle of a nasty divorce and didn't care how much money she spent; whatever she wanted, regardless of the cost, she got. In fact, it was rumored her husband Ted Ammon, had allotted several millions of dollars to remodel the immense dwelling that was to be hers and their children's primary residence after the divorce. They needed a good electrician, Dan's friend said, and felt that Danny would be the perfect man for the job. Danny decided he would go into the city the next day to check this out for himself and meet with the wealthy Mrs. Ammon. The story sounded like an exaggerated tale to me. I would find out in less than twenty-four hours, it wasn't.

Danny called me on the way home from the city ecstatic that he got the job and he would be making a lot of money. He sounded like a kid let loose in a candy shop. I couldn't help but get caught up in Dan's fervor. This could be the chance to really get us out of a financial hole and do some much-needed work on our house. Dan quit the job he had recently obtained and started his new employment in New York City that following Monday morning. In a matter of weeks, Danny was promoted from electrician to head electrician to Project Manager. According to Dan, Generosa Ammon was impressed with his work. He advanced from being paid by the hour to a yearly salary and was making more than he ever imagined he could make. Dan traveled back and forth to the city like hundreds of other commuters. But after a few weeks of inching along on the Long Island Expressway, he decided he was going to stay in the city, sleep in his truck and come home on the weekend. I wasn't thrilled with this idea and didn't make a big deal about it until I found out that Generosa Ammon took it upon herself to make the arrangements for Danny to stay at the same swank hotel that she was living in while waiting for her luxurious apartment building to be complete. I had already discovered that Generosa Ammon was not 'some dumb old rich broad,' like Danny said. Quite the contrary. Generosa was an attractive shapely blonde, only a few years older than I was. She was intelligent, cultured and used to getting her way. Danny assured me it wasn't what I thought. I knew I wasn't going to win, so I didn't fight it even though little red flags were popping up all over the place. Generosa was a woman of wealth and power – and she was single. She had left Ted months before after believing he had been carrying on an affair while she was living in their castle in England and he was working in New York. As the story goes, she went straight to her attorneys and filed a divorce demanding a huge chunk of Ted's reported wealth. Even with knowing this, I convinced myself this was the financial opportunity of a lifetime. I couldn't believe half of what Danny told me anyway, but money did start coming in, not in the form of currency in my hand, but in lavish ridiculous gifts. Every weekend it was something else. Something extravagant and unnecessary. If Generosa was out to spend every last penny of Ted's money she found a bottomless pit in Danny.

Danny had always outdone himself on Christmas regardless of whether we had money or not. The Christmas Eve of 2000 was beyond anyone's imagination. Danny must have made half a dozen trips to his car hauling in enormous boxes. Our family and friends stood at the door whooping and hollering like a bunch of contestants on a game show cheering Danny on with every armload of boxes and gift bags he carried in. He filled the entire living room and dining area with expensively wrapped packages. I received more jewelry that night than most women acquire in a lifetime. After everyone said their goodbyes and happily carried out their mountain of gifts, Danny told me to come into the living room and sit down. He had something special for me. He handed me an envelope with two roundtrip tickets to the Bahamas and reservations from December 28 through December 31 at one of the famous hotels. I was speechless. My mind leaped to a second honeymoon. This was surely Danny's way of making up. How wrong I was. The second ticket was not for him, but for my dear friend Joy who lives in Florida. It took a few moments for me to compute that it was Joy and I who were going to the Bahamas, not Danny and I. Danny planned every detail including meeting Joy at the Orlando Airport, limousine service to Miami, and the flight to the Bahamas. He even threw in five thousand dollars. This was way more than red flags; this was colossal flashing neon lights. I called my mother first thing Christmas morning in hopes she could offer some advice on whether or not I should accept Danny's outlandish offer. The news wasn't quite as crushing to my mother. There wasn't anything Danny could do that would shock her. She basically said to go ahead and enjoy myself. The way she looked at it, staying at home wasn't going to change Danny's course of action.

It took Joy and I over fourteen hours to get to the Bahamas to stay for only two and a half days, but it was worth it. Neither one of us ever had any money to just be frivolous. We strolled around the famous Atlantis casino as giddy as two kids at a carnival gaping at the assortment of machines and flashing neon lights. Much to our delight, Joy's first quarter in the slot machine won her a twenty-five-hundred-dollar jackpot. My dear kooky friend thought she broke the machine when the sirens went off and the lights flashed. She was still in a daze when she collected her winnings. Joy stuffed her grand prize in her pocketbook, hid her purse under her jacket, grabbed my arm, and ushered me out the door and back to our hotel room where she slept with her pocketbook under her pillow, she wasn't going to take any chances. It was a short but much-needed few days for both of us. In less than twenty-four hours a heavy dose of reality was waiting for me. It would be a long time before I would experience any gaiety.

We were back at Joy's house a few hours before New Year's Eve. I called Danny using the excuse that I wanted to tell him about Joy's windfall. Of course, what I really wanted was to find out what he was doing and with whom. Danny answered his cell on the first ring. There was a lot of commotion in the background. I had to tell him three times it was me on the phone, which I found extremely irritating since my own cell phone number should have appeared on his cell screen. I barely had a chance to say hello before he cut me short and put my daughter on the phone. She was bubbly and chattered about this gorgeous hotel they were staying at and how her father's nice boss Generosa was with them and that she was paying for everything. Personally, I didn't care a hoot who was paying for what. What I did care about was why *that* woman was celebrating New Year's Eve with *my* family. Danny conveniently never got back on the phone. I watched the New Year come in sitting around the television at Joy's parent's home, silently fuming. I wound up stuck in Florida for an additional day because all flights along the eastern seaboard were delayed due to severe weather conditions. So, I did what most women would do under the circumstances, I shopped. Joy and I spent a full day spending the money that was left from our trip.

Danny picked me up at the LaGuardia Airport looking quite spiffy in a new and rather expensive-looking black leather jacket, black pants and a beige mock turtleneck. In a matter of days, Danny had transformed from a blue-collar, dirt-under-the-nails electrician into some spurious manicured individual I did not know. After seeing him dressed to the nines and strutting as if he were a model for some sultry cologne advertisement, I was secretly glad I spent every penny of the money he gave me. My spiteful bitchiness may not have altered the rapid development between Danny and Generosa, but it did give me a moment of satisfaction.

Danny talked non-stop from the moment we left the airport, pretending to be interested in my trip to the Bahamas and Joy's triumph at the slot machine. He was good at flapping his lips about nothing of any importance, a tactic of his to keep me at bay. Whenever I attempted to switch the conversation to what I wanted to hear, such as why I was sent to the Bahamas and what Generosa was doing with my family on New Year's Eve, he tip-toed around the question or completely avoided answering it altogether. He would have made a great politician. Dan had a knack for twisting the truth, double-talking and skirting any issue that might have put him on the hot seat. Usually, by the time you were done speaking with Dan, *you* were apologizing to him for something *he* did. I refused to let Danny railroad me. I knew something was going on between him and his boss and I wanted Danny to be upfront and admit his guilt. I don't know why I expected that. He was never honest before. He only told me about Beth to hurt her, not to come clean with me. When I persisted in my pathetic interrogation, I was met with the usual response, 'it was all in my head.' I didn't give up in my pursuit. For three months I was on a mental mission, possessed with finding something that would prove that Danny was having an affair with Generosa. It was the first weekend of March when I had the opportunity to search through Danny's wallet while he was in the shower. I found the mother lode - not one, not two, but three incriminating receipts from a few days before. One for firewood, one for wine, one for steaks, all purchased from shops in East Hampton where Generosa had her country estate. In a matter of seconds, I composed a cozy little scene in my mind for the cheating lovers, wood for the blazing fire, wine in long-stemmed crystal glasses, and medium-rare filet mignon smothered in baby pearl onions and shiitake mushrooms to boost their energy. After they had non-stop sex on a plush white bear rug in front of a twenty-foot stone fireplace. It's a pity I wasted some of my best fantasizing on two undeserving individuals.

Talk about déjà vu. I felt as if I was back in 1997 ready to tear the shower curtain back just as I had done when I found the message from Beth on Dan's beeper. But I didn't. I was more experienced now. I waited. The moment he stepped out of the bathroom, I attacked. If I were a Pitbull I would have sunk my fangs around his throat. But Dan was just as cool, calm and collected as he was three years before. He told me those receipts indicated nothing. He was her employee and she asked him to deliver these items to her East Hampton home. The good employee that he was, he did as he was told. Dan was such a master at turning my mind around that he once again succeeded in making me doubt myself. The story sounded plausible. He was her employee. He could have bought those items for her and delivered them to the house. Receipts didn't necessarily mean they were having an affair. Four months later I discovered my instincts were right. It happened the day we returned from a family vacation to Disney in April of 2001, a vacation I called the trip from hell. Throughout the vacation Danny was on his cell phone whispering, murmuring and chuckling under his breath. When I questioned him, he answered that he was running the business long distance. I know Danny had the ability to twist and distort my mind, but I wasn't a complete idiot. No one takes care of business by whispering sweet nothings to their workers. I knew he was talking to *HER*. I was jealous, resentful, bitter and downright miserable. I couldn't wait to leave. But home offered me no comfort. About two weeks before the trip from hell, I had come home from work and found my house gutted. Danny was having my house renovated, purely from guilt. Walls had been knocked down, kitchen cabinets were broken to pieces, electrical wires hung from rafters, and the roof was *gone*. A huge blue tarp was tied down over the house like a deflated air balloon. I had asked for a new kitchen, not a new house. Danny told me he was building me my dream home - fireplace, front porch, skylights and all. I was horrified and too overwhelmed with the disaster to be happy. An enormous dumpster took up most of the driveway and was filled with piles of broken sheetrock, cracked studs with protruding rusted nails, and on top of the rubbish pile was my sink and stove! There were piles of garbage everywhere. I had no idea what happened to my dishes, pots, pans and utensils. Sawdust covered the entire house, in the bedrooms, closets and even on the dogs. There wasn't a clean towel in sight.

I had hoped I would return to some progress, but the house was in the same disheveled and unsightly mess that I left. Light bulbs still dangled off wires, furniture was toppled over covered with dusty sheets of plastic, and my gutted kitchen remained gutted. I lived like this for months, not able to cook a simple meal or even make a cup of coffee; the coffee maker was thrown out with everything else that was on the counter. I don't know if I will ever fully understand why I subjected my family to live the way we did, except to say that I was emotionally battered and numb to my surroundings.

Unlike other people that come home from a trip, relax with a cup of coffee and ponder the highlights of their vacation, I had to fight my way through the dust and dirt and depression. The kids darted off to their friends as soon as the car rolled into the driveway. Danny helped me bring the luggage in and told me he was leaving. My stomach rose up to my chest and then, like a roller coaster, plummeted suddenly. It wasn't what he said but the way he said it. Words didn't need to be articulated in fluent detail, a megaphone couldn't have been any louder or clearer. He was leaving and he wasn't coming back. I pleaded, literally down on all fours. I clung to his leg like a crying child. It's shameful to admit that I begged him to change his mind. But my words fell on deaf ears. He took his new suitcase full of name-brand clothes and abandoned me like the old socks that he left behind in his bureau drawer. He deserted me on the floor as if I were nothing more to him than a broken useless toy.

I would like to believe that Danny felt some remorse. Whether it was remorse or guilt, he called my brother to come over and check on me in case I did something drastic to myself. I was still crumpled on the hallway floor when my brother got to my house. He sat down next to me, held my hand and offered his standard line of consolation that he recited to me over the years - that I was young, I had an entire life ahead of me, I'd get over it. Or words to that effect. When you're in a state of despair there is very little anyone can say to lift your spirits. Maybe somewhere in the back of your mind you know that time heals all wounds, but when you're in the moment, there is no future time. There is only the present painful moment. My brother stayed with me for over an hour, until he felt it was safe for him to leave me alone. I wasn't going to do anything to myself. I was more than angry, I was hurt. Angry with myself for being a complete fool. I had taken enough psychology courses over the years to know what I should and should not have done. I certainly knew what I might have suggested to someone else, yet I was trapped in my own way. It was the same pattern for almost twenty years of marriage, I would cry like a little girl and beg Dan to stay, then sob some more and take him back. I knew this time no amount of crying or begging on my knees would keep Danny home. Generosa was a woman Danny would stick with; I could not compete with her wealth and her power. I remained in a self-pitied stupor until the sun was nearly down. Eventually, I removed myself off the filthy floor covered with sawdust and scattered with bent nails.

Dan officially moved in with Generosa and her children at the ritzy New York hotel. I saw little of him, except for the days when he would ride out from the city for my younger son's Little League game. Seeing him was difficult enough, but what really infuriated me was Generosa, her children and her dog right along with Dan. I was outraged that she had the audacity to show up at my son's game; we weren't even divorced yet. To make matters worse my kids began to spend time with their father and his girlfriend. On Father's Day

Danny picked the kids up and they happily trounced off to Generosa's East Hampton home; the million-dollar estate that was to be hers as part of her divorce settlement. I was left alone in my empty broken house to wallow in self-pity. I forced myself to go outside and get some fresh air. I was sitting on my half-finished front porch attempting to enjoy the warm day when the two Rottweilers from down the road got loose from their property. They ran past my house and headed for my neighbor's tiny Maltese innocently bathing in the sunshine. I numbly watched that horrible unforgettable scene as they mauled the little dog and ran off with its lifeless body clenched in the jaws of the bigger dog's mouth. I spent the remainder of the afternoon talking with the police and consoling my elderly neighbor. The tragic event sunk me deeper into a dismal gloom. For several weeks I played the gruesome image in my mind like a remote stuck on rewind. About a week or so after that dreadful day, Danny brought me a taser gun, also known as a stun gun, for protection. I had never heard of such a device before. He told me to zap the Rottweilers if they came on my property. But the dogs were impounded the same day they mauled the little dog. Even if the animals were still around, I wanted nothing to do with this weapon and was terrified my sons would get their hands on it. I hid it in the basement and forgot about it, unknowing that the infamous stun gun would become a target of incessant questioning and harassment.

My bitterness and resentment deepened over the summer of 2001. I resented that my children seemed to have forgiven their father and were happy to spend nearly every day at the East Hampton country home rather than with me. It was upsetting to see my children so impressed with Generosa's wealth, her castle in England, the nannies she had for her children and the way their father lavishly spent *her* money.

Each time my kids returned home from a visit they had another tale of extravagance to tell me.

I knew it was common to feel hurt and rejected when your children spend time with the opposite parent and that parent's new significant other. I've had many friends that had gone through divorces and shared their stories with me, but I had no idea how jealous and bitter I would be. Maintaining my calm was a daily challenge. I had to grit my teeth and bite my tongue to keep from lashing out at my children. I wasn't always successful.

Eventually, my kids got bored with the extravagance. Their family outings to East Hampton ended before the summer was over.

MURDER, MEDIA AND MAYHEM

"Do not be anxious about tomorrow, tomorrow will look after itself."
~ The Bible

My youngest son's eleventh birthday came five weeks after the terrifying attack of September 11, which was only five months from when Danny left. It was a terribly frightening time for everyone, especially children. My little boy had not understood the turmoil of his parents' marriage or why his father was gone. He was too young to know about his father's mysterious periodic disappearances or his extramarital affairs. He simply knew his father as the person who taught him how to ride a bike and hook a worm. Dan was his dad, the man who strapped on his skies, tied his ice skates and fit him for his first baseball mitt. When his father left, a big piece of my son went with him.

On the morning of his birthday, my eleven-year-old was up early eagerly waiting for his father to come to take him out for breakfast. He had expected they would spend the whole day together, but when Danny dropped him off after their meal, he told his son he couldn't stay because he had to attend his cousin's wedding. He promised him he'd be back later for birthday cake, which I knew was one of Danny's lies to cover his guilt. My son pestered me all day when his father was coming back. I was furious that Danny would make a promise he couldn't keep. Unfortunately, I took my anger out on my little guy. It broke my heart to see this little boy run to the window every time he heard a car on the road. Each time the phone rang Tony grabbed it off its hook expecting his father to be on the other end. Danny finally called to say there was a delay with the wedding and he wasn't sure if he could make it in time for the cake. The only one that was surprised was Tony. I watched his little boy face instantly change from hopefulness to sadness.

Later in the afternoon my brother and his family and one of Tony's friends gathered for a small birthday celebration. Tony wouldn't let us have the cake until Danny got there, but by seven o'clock when it was evident that his father wasn't going to be joining us, we sang Happy Birthday as the birthday boy cheerlessly blew out his candles. After my family left, I stomped around throwing paper party dishes in the garbage with a vengeance. By eight-thirty I needed to take Tony's friend home. I was halfway down the road when Danny turned onto the street. I half-heartedly drove back to the house with an obvious chip on my shoulder. Tony's own eagerness to see his father had faded beneath his hurt and anger. Danny carefully avoided eye contact with me and directed his conversation to his son. Since Danny did manage to make it back to the house, I asked him, none too sweetly I might add, if he could take a look at the leak in Tony's closet, the same leak he said he would fix a few weeks ago. When the upstairs addition was added on, water leaked in when it rained and it had been raining a lot. I had wedged a plastic bag in the crevice, but my handy work was not all that handy and the rain came in on Tony's clothes. I left Danny at the house in his fancy suit plugging up the leak while I proceeded to take Tony's friend back home. To my surprise, my son came with me. I had expected that he would want to stay with his father. I assumed Danny would still be there when we returned, but par for the course, he wasn't. He slipped into the night without so much as a goodbye or a hug for his son. When Tony came to the sad conclusion that his father was gone for the night, he plopped on his bed and refused to talk with anyone.

The day after Tony's birthday Danny called me in the morning at work sounding upset, Ted Ammon was found dead. It was believed to be an overdose of some kind. Generosa was due to sign their divorce papers that weekend. It wasn't until the next day that it was reported that he was brutally murdered. I had never met Mr. Ammon and I certainly was not fond of Generosa, but my immediate reaction was how horrible this would be for their children. Their twins were the same age as Tony. I never considered Danny or Generosa as suspects, particularly not Danny, but the law and the media had other thoughts, especially since word was out that Ted Ammon never changed his will. Everything was left to Generosa.

The onslaught of the media began around Halloween. My father-in-law had stopped over while I was in the middle of painting the front door. We were inside talking when there was a knock on the door; my hands were full of red paint so my father-in-law answered it. A medium-built man with light brown hair was holding a small notepad in his hand; he introduced himself as a reporter from the *New York Post*. He wanted to know if Danny was available and if he would mind making a statement. I asked the reporter what he wanted a statement about, but my father-in-law interrupted. He made it clear to the reporter that Danny was not there and no one had anything to say. He firmly closed the door with the reporter standing on the front porch, notepad in hand. Dan's father advised me not to talk to anyone until we found out what was going on. What went on was a rapid progression of the media, scores of phone calls from TV stations and every newspaper, including one from London. They were all hoping for the same thing, that Danny would make a public announcement of his whereabouts on the night Theodore Ammon was murdered. Neither Danny nor Generosa ever made a public statement; the two of them were conveniently protected by Generosa's attorneys. My children and I were not as lucky. I was in the bathroom putting my makeup on getting ready for an event at my job when my older son came running into the house out of breath. He told me there were men with cameras on their shoulders that followed him from the bus stop. I peered out the window and was astounded to see an entourage of reporters mulling around the front of my house, vans from CBS, NBC, ABC and Channel 12 News were parked along the road. I was looking out at them, and they were ogling back at me. I was concerned that the newscasters would hound Tony when he got off the school bus. Little Dan and I planned to run to my car and speed off before the reporters could catch us so I could pick Tony up directly from school and hide out at my mother's. But the reporters stormed at me the moment I opened my door, clicking their cameras in my face demanding to know if I had a statement and if I thought Danny committed the murder. I watched them from the rearview mirror taking pictures of my car driving down the road. Almost every afternoon hordes of reporters were waiting for me. Cameras clicked and clacked non-stop as I ran to my house covering my face with my hands. I called Danny's younger brother, a New York City cop. Thankfully he was at home. He was at my house in record-breaking time and called the local police. I hid in the house trembling, nearly gnawing my fingernails down while my brother-in-law spoke to the cops. Unfortunately, there wasn't anything the police could do. The reporters were shrewd enough to know that as long as no one was on my property, they weren't breaking any laws. Danny's brother, a big hulk of a guy, but gentle as a lamb, asked them nicely to leave my family alone. They did on that day, but they would be back again and again for months to come. Neither my children nor myself stayed in our house any longer than we had to. Straight from work, I'd pick the boys up from school and drove them to their friends. My daughter went to her boyfriend's house right from work. I took to hiding at my mother's and wouldn't pick up my boys until I was sure the reporters weren't around, then my daughter would come home. When we were safe within the confine of our home, the two older kids would close themselves into their rooms and Tony would fall asleep in my bed with the TV on. What little family life we had, had totally disintegrated.

When the reporters discovered they weren't going to get anywhere with me, they invaded my neighbors. They swarmed the neighborhood asking personal questions about Danny and our marriage. For a while the media retreated, only to be replaced by detectives. They started at Carol's house. Two detectives asked her husband to come to the precinct for questioning. Being one of Danny's closest friends, Greg had worked for Danny on Generosa's New York City apartment. He also helped to install an alarm system at the East Hampton house, the same alarm system that was mysteriously turned off on the night Mr. Ammon was murdered. The detectives questioned Greg for over three hours. Later that day, the same two detectives knocked on my door. They also grilled me for hours, not at the precinct, but on my front porch so that any neighbor passing my house could witness the interrogation. They repeated the same questions over and over again wanting to know Danny's whereabouts on the weekend of October twentieth to twenty-first and whether Danny ever gave me anything for protection.

Occasionally I caught myself stammering. I didn't want the detectives to think I was hiding anything. It wasn't as if I was accustomed to standing on my front porch being probed by two burly intimidating detectives about the possibility that my husband could have murdered another individual. This wasn't a scene from Law & Order and it wasn't the autumn cold that caused my body to tremble and my teeth to chatter. The younger taller detective handed me his card. Under his name in bold print was the word **Homicide**. *Homicide!* The word alone was unnerving. He told me to call him if I remembered anything. I could barely recall what I had for dinner the night before. I waited until I saw the detective's car turn onto the main road, then zoomed to my mother's house. I showed my mother the card and told her the questions the detectives kept asking me. Mom and I on occasion thought the unthinkable, but neither of us would believe that Danny was responsible for the murder. It was inconceivable.

Christmas Eve of 2001 was a sad replica of the previous year. Carol and her family and my brother's family were at my house for our traditional holiday gathering. There was some question as to whether Danny would show up, or if he would find some excuse as he did for Tony's birthday. He strolled in near midnight, not with the usual array of gifts, but enough for everyone. The laughter and gaiety of Christmases past was nothing more than a bittersweet memory. The relationship between Danny and his close friend Greg changed after the detectives interrogated him. That would put a damper on any friendship. Finding a subject that would not trigger questions about the murder was a challenge. My brother told a few jokes that led to a few laughs, but most of the evening was awkward for all of us. Surprisingly Danny stayed the night. I had expected he would have left after an hour or so and head back to his new family. When everyone had left, he sprawled out on the couch as if he still lived there, and was snoring by the time I washed my face. I wrapped myself in a big comforter and curled up on the loveseat across from him and studied his face as he slept, trying to figure out what it was that kept me bound to him. An interesting analogy popped into my mind while I watched the fire gradually burn down, I was like those few stubborn embers that refused to die out.

Christmas breakfast was quiet and uneasy. Danny made small talk with the kids; every once in a while, one of them chuckled at an attempted joke. I cooked breakfast while Danny paced the floor. I knew from his nervous laugh that he wanted to leave but didn't know how to say it. I wasn't about to give him the green light. I let him squirm. He gobbled down his breakfast and handed the kids an additional hundred dollars each, his way of making up for the fact that he would not be having Christmas dinner with them. He wished them a Merry Christmas and left, not with his usual swaggering walk, more subdued I thought, even sad, or maybe I was projecting my feelings onto him.

The post-holiday blues lingered well into January. I couldn't sleep and when I did I couldn't get out of bed in the morning. I found myself not paying attention to what I was doing or where I was driving. I'd pass exits or slam on the brakes at a traffic light.

Work wasn't my haven as it had been in the past. I was edgy and irritable and snapped at simple questions from co-workers. I wasn't able to focus and kept forgetting what I did with my paperwork. When I entered a room, I couldn't remember what it was I needed. I exhibited the classic signs of stress, but the real stress hadn't even hit yet. The year 2002 didn't appear any more promising than the previous. And by far it wasn't. There's a saying that goes, 'what else can happen?' – don't say it. Don't even put the thought out there, because believe me, anything can happen.

I had dragged my body out of bed on a cold Thursday morning on January 24, 2002 feeling even more exhausted than usual. I hadn't fully absorbed the fact that my divorce was finalized the day before. It was my attorney who called to give me the startling news. He was very surprised that the divorce went through so fast. The entire divorce process from the initial submission of paperwork to receiving the stamped sealed documents took only four months, an unusually short amount of time in the state of New York. I had shuffled from the kitchen to the dining area in my worn slippers and unrolled the morning newspaper. My eyes were still heavy from a sleepless night, but they sprang open as if I had stuck my finger in a live electrical outlet. On the front page of *Newsday*, in big letters – DANNY AND AMMON'S WIDOW MARRY! The fury and rage that rose up from my gut was indescribable. Danny never gave any indication that he was planning on getting married, for me to discover this information through the newspaper no less, and to do this only one day after our own divorce, seemed unconscionable. I called him every name under the sun. I was shaking so much I could barely hold the paper. The newspapers had a field day with the story. They loved that Danny wed the wealthy widow twenty-four hours after our marital contract was terminated. For me to learn that Danny was honeymooning at Generosa's castle in England to protect *her* children from the media, nearly gave me a stroke. There certainly was no way I could protect my children from their father's thoughtless and selfish act; it wasn't just me that Danny hurt.

The boy's alarm clock went off, but I had no intention of getting them up and sending them to school. I didn't see how either of them would be able to concentrate once they found out their father had gotten married. I sent Rachelle to their bedroom to shut the alarm off. The longer they stayed asleep, the better. I had let the dogs out the back door to do their morning business, but instead of running to the backyard as they normally did, they ran toward the front barking wildly. I peeked out and discovered that the press had already congregated in front of my house. I knew that as soon as one of us opened the door they would attack like sharks on a fresh kill. I made a decision that all of us would stay home. When my sons got up, the four of us huddled around the kitchen table. Tony, too young to understand the full impact, was happy for a day off from school but asked, as only an innocent child would, if this meant his father was never moving back in with us.

Little Dan on the other hand was angry. He took Danny's sneaky marriage as a personal betrayal. I couldn't provide answers to their questions. Within the hour the phone began to ring, first from family and friends wanting to know if I heard the stunning news. By lunch, an overwhelming number of calls came from every newspaper, news station and magazine. I finally stopped answering the calls and had to change the message on my answering machine. The new message stated that I had no comment to make regarding the current headlines and to please respect my family's privacy. I turned the ringer off. Throughout the day the light continued to flash on my machine. The kids and I hid in the house all day. I wouldn't let them answer the phone, go near a window or out of the house. No one came over in fear of being trapped by the press. We were prisoners in our own home. Later that evening while we were watching television, the news flashed on. There was my house on the TV! The newscaster was showing the public the average-sized Long Island home that Danny left for the expansive castle he would be living at in England. My family might as well have lived in a glass house, our every move was noted. Whenever Danny's name hit the press, and it hit the press often, reporters were at my door. It was up to me to protect my children and fight for my family's privacy.

The detectives were at my house every few days. They harped on the same questions, never letting up, persistent and unflagging in their relentless attempt to wear me down the way a constant drip of water eventually bores a hole through dense stone. Their tireless pursuit didn't stop with me; they went so far as to track down a former job of my mother's. One of the women in the office that she remained close with knew what was going on and called to tell her two homicide detectives flashed their badges, asked questions of where they might find her and left their calling card. Unfortunately, there were other women in the organization who weren't aware my mother had a connection, however slight, to the current headlines. I don't know if the detectives were embarrassed when they learned my mother hadn't worked there in over five years, but my mother certainly was. My mother was understandably annoyed that near-strangers were privy to what was going on in our family's lives. My mother didn't go around blabbing that Danny was her son-in-law, former or otherwise. It wasn't a topic that was discussed outside of family and close friends. Fearful that the detectives would pursue their search and show up at my mother's new place of business, she called the number on the card. They asked my mother several of the same questions they asked me, apparently convinced that Danny had confessed to me and that I in turn confided to my mother.

The steady strain had taken its toll on my family. The more Danny's name appeared in the papers, the more we retreated into our own worlds. The more the finger was pointed at Danny, the more we denied it. We slowly fell apart. None of us could sleep. We were like zombies roaming around the house bumping into each other at all hours of the night. We'd finally fall into a deep sleep as the sun was coming up. It had become a daily battle to get the boys off to school. Half the time I was successful, the other half they refused to get out of bed. I was too tired to argue with them. Naturally, their grades plummeted. Everyone was short-tempered; one wrong word and we'd attack one another like dogs in a pit. When my sons finally did wake up, they disappeared to their friends. They wanted to be anywhere but home. Rachelle stayed more and more at her boyfriend's. Thankfully his parents were kind and understanding. Except for the holiday meals, we never shared dinner together. We were like nomads, never in one place too long. We scattered in different directions.

Everyday I'd haul my body out of bed, mechanically dab on some make-up and drive to work. Regardless of the fact that I was close with the girls who worked with me, I was too mortified and embarrassed to speak with anyone and spent as much time as I could hiding out in my office. I ventured out of my safe little cubicle only when absolutely necessary. I feared that the parents who entrusted their children to my care would connect my last name to the one that continued to make the headlines.

I couldn't cope with the onslaught of publicity that caused my children and myself endless shame and disgrace. I began having panic attacks to the degree that I often needed to pull my car over to the side of the road because I swore, I was having a heart attack. I'd cry endlessly whenever I was alone, whether in my car or folding laundry. My face was one continual puffy, blotched mess that I attempted to cover with extra layers of make-up. I wasn't fooling anyone. On the evening that I picked the kids up at counseling, (I at least made sure that they received some help), their therapist took me on the side and told me I needed help too. She gave me the name of a psychiatrist who could prescribe something to help me cope. I cried some more. I had lost control of my life. I was a failure as a mother. I felt like a paralyzed person, able to see what was going on around me but incapable of responding. I had never taken a drug of any sort in my life, except for the occasional antibiotic or Tylenol. I never dabbled in mind-altering drugs. Drugs terrified me. I didn't even smoke. The counselor pushed the psychiatrist's card in my hand and reminded me how much my children needed a mother. I stuck it in my purse. It was a full two weeks before I called for an appointment and that was only after I woke during the night with severe tightness in my chest as if someone was crushing my ribs in a vice. I was given a prescription for Xanax. Miraculously, the pains in my chest subsided. I was nearly functional.

On the morning of March 30, 2002, I was overjoyed that a repairman was at my house fixing the heat. Although the thermostat registered less than sixty degrees, I was feeling pretty good. I think my daily dose of the little pink pills had much to do with the ability to function. I wasn't suffering from panic attacks or burying my head in my pillows crying. Not to say that life was a bowl of cherries. Detectives continued to show up at my door, and I definitely hadn't adjusted to Danny's disingenuous marriage to Princess Ta Ta, my nickname for Generosa. But on that sunny Saturday morning, I answered the phone with a cheerful voice. My lightheartedness was short-lived. My former sister-in-law was on the phone. Danny's younger brother, the police officer who did his best to keep the news reporters at bay, had been rushed to the hospital in cardiac arrest, a few hours later he died. My legs buckled under with this dreadful news, I slid, more like slithered, down the front of the kitchen cabinet, knocking the dog's water bowl over. Slumped against the cabinet, sitting in a puddle of cold water, I wailed for the loss of someone dear. The kids were woken by the mournful sobs that rose from deep within my soul. The repairmen made a quiet exit. The news was shocking to everyone. He wasn't sick. He wasn't old. He was a strong hulking man, a New York police officer; a huggable big bear of a guy with a broad happy smile known for his easy-going manner and his ability to get people to laugh. He was the stable one, the rock, the person other family members depended on, the mediator, the referee, the arbitrator, the hero. His death was a tremendous loss to the Pelosi family and to the community as well. A hundred or more uniformed police and firemen donning black armbands for their fallen comrade led a solemn procession of police cars, fire trucks and scores of vehicles from the funeral parlor to the cemetery. The press remarkably kept their distance during that sorrowful time, although a few days after his death, a story or two was printed in an effort to link Danny's brother in some way to the crime. There had been unfounded reports that he had obstructed justice in an attempt to protect his older brother. The death of Danny's brother would become a major cause of contention within the Pelosi family and a shocking strategy that the prosecuting attorney targeted two years later at Danny's trial.

A few weeks after the funeral, around the second weekend of April, I attended a weekend seminar with my dear friend Josephine at the Omega conference in New York City. It was an intense two days of lectures from well-known spiritual leaders that covered topics from healing to connecting to God.

With everything that had been taking place in my life, Josephine thought of me when she heard about the conference and made all the arrangements for the both of us to attend. Josephine is a psychic medium. Through Josephine's loving guidance and the incredibly enlightening weekend, I was able to understand that although my brother-in-law was no longer on the earth plane, in 'spirit' he would be my guiding light.

Coincidentally or not (I have since learned there are no coincidences), on Sunday night when I returned from the conference weekend, I received a call from a relative. She told me about a dream she had the night before. In the dream Danny's brother called her into a room where there was an old-fashioned record player; he told her to play the record "Wind Beneath My Wings" by Bette Midler. In the dream, he said, "Tell Tami that song is for her." In the months following his death, whenever I was feeling down, frightened or overwhelmed, Bette Midler's 'Wind Beneath My Wings,' would *coincidentally* play on the radio, confirming what Josephine told me. I'd often find myself "talking" to my brother-in-law, asking for his help, but I didn't trust that he heard my prayers. I asked him for a sign, some assurance that he truly was there. A little voice suggested that whenever I would find a penny, I could trust my prayers were being heard. Not three days after I made this little agreement with my deceased brother-in-law, I arrived at work one morning and found a jar filled with pennies that had been left anonymously on the center's doorstep! Eighty dollars' worth! An inordinate number of pennies have continued to mysteriously pop up in the oddest places and at the most needed times.

I came to learn that my experience with pennies wasn't as unique as I believed it was. When I shared the connection that pennies had for me, I was surprised at how many others had similar tales to tell. I related to one story in particular about a woman who when worried or fearful inevitably finds a coin, not necessarily a penny. She believes it's a message from God since all coins have *In God We Trust* inscribed on them. For her, it's a time to take a moment to pray and to acknowledge that God is always with her. I like that story.

I was fond of Danny's brother, everyone was. He was a wonderful caring individual who was often a source of support during some of the difficult times of my marriage. Ironically, it was through his death that I felt most connected to him. Each time a penny magically appeared I could envision my brother-in-law's warm smile and feel a sense of peaceful comfort settle around me. When we take notice, messages of encouragement come to us in the most unusual of ways.

2002

INTERROGATED, INTIMATED

"Though I walk in the midst of trouble, you preserve my life; you stretch out your hand against the anger of my foes, with you right hand you save me."
~ Psalm 138:7

One warm Saturday evening in mid-June my son Tony and I were watching a video. We sat with a huge bowl of popcorn in between the two of us, taking turns shoving our hands in the mound of hot buttery popped corn and stuffing handfuls in our mouths. It was one of the few occasions that I almost believed my life was as normal as any other American family. Like other American families with teenagers, a knock on the door at nine-thirty in the evening sets your heart pumping. Terrified that I might open the door to a uniformed police officer asking if I was the mother of such and such, I switched the dim overhead porch light on with my heart in my mouth. I was relieved on one hand that it wasn't police officers with some dreadful news but shocked to find the same two detectives back on my front porch at that hour of the night. I took a quick look over my shoulder to see if Tony had followed me, then stepped outside and quietly closed the door behind me. The detectives kept their voices low, whether out of consideration or intimidation I'm not sure. Hastily they went through their formal preliminaries and immediately went about shooting questions at me like a loaded automatic rifle.

"Did Danny ever give me anything for protection?"

"Did he leave the house with any items on that Sunday night?"

"Did I leave Danny in the house when I left?"

"Was he alone in the house?"

"Was anything missing after he left?"

They demanded I go over every detail of the weekend of Tony's birthday. The detectives insisted I knew more than I was telling them and that I was purposely withholding information. They threatened that I had better realize what I was doing and get out of my denial and face the fact that my ex-husband was a murderer and I had better tell my kids.

I heard a little noise behind me and turned to catch my eleven-year-old son's face pressing against the window screen. I had no idea how much of this interrogation he had heard. He whispered to me that my mother was on the phone. Believing that was his excuse for eavesdropping, I urged him to go back to watching the movie and assured him I'd be inside shortly. But I was not. My young child's frightened face at the window did not deter the plainclothesmen. They continued where they left off without regard for my child. I was tormented for what seemed like hours. When they did leave, they forewarned that they would be back as often as they deemed necessary. In the middle of this impromptu interrogation, I saw my mother's car slowly drive past my house, go down the road and not return. I found out later that she had called and when Tony told her I was outside talking to some men, she rushed to my house. Unsure of what she should do when she saw the three of us on the front porch, she parked across from my neighbor's house and waited until she saw their car turn the corner before coming to my house. We sat outside on the porch step for a few minutes. In a low whisper, I briefed her on what the detectives had threatened. Other than that, we were silent. After my mother left, still shaken by the evening's event, I managed to get to the bathroom in time to vomit. I did my best to compose myself before going into the den with my son and answered his questions without lying but also without frightening him. Tony might have only been eleven years old, but he wasn't an idiot. Children are a lot wiser than adults give them credit for. I could have lied until I was blue in the face to shield him from what was taking place in his father's life and in our lives, but all he would need to do was look at a newspaper, turn the television on or have some half-brain make a stupid comment that his father was a murderer. There was no way to protect my family from this horrible mess. I was at least grateful the two older ones weren't around to bear witness to that particular daunting event.

Early the next morning my mother called and strongly advised me to get a lawyer. She believed the detectives were harassing me and I needed legal protection. I didn't feel I had anything to hide. But my mother was adamant. She worried that they would arrest me, which I thought was far-fetched; even so, I called the lawyer that I used for my divorce later that day. He contacted homicide and informed them he was representing me. He explained I had nothing to hide and that I was willing to speak with them, but in the future, he would be present.

Miracles of miracles, the detectives stopped coming to my house and never asked me to come in for questioning. But every couple of days they would drive up and down the road, just to let me know they hadn't gone away. They were watching.

Sometime during the summer, a friend who is a landscaper was doing some work on my property. He mentioned that a couple of electricians had come to the house that morning and needed to go into the basement to check on some wiring. He told me he let them in and that they were in the basement for several hours. I called Danny pissed that he was giving strangers permission to go in my house when I wasn't home; we had had an agreement that he would let me know when workers would be at my house. But Danny said he didn't send any electricians and swore that he didn't know who was in my basement. He told me he would look into it. I didn't like that Danny seemed nervous and decided it might be best to contact my attorney. My lawyer was concerned that it might have been undercover cops planting listening devices in my house and advised me to be careful of what I said on the phone. I was outraged that the detectives would go to any length to try and 'catch' me in a lie and prove themselves right. This was a total invasion of my privacy. It was unsettling what the law could do and get away with. When the kids came home from school, I took them outside; we went for a walk down the road, away from my house, far away from the listening devices so I could tell them what was going on. I felt like a criminal, like I *was* hiding something. The kids were terrified. We were afraid to talk on the phone; frightened we might say something that may sound incriminating. We nearly tiptoed around the house. We searched for anything that remotely resembled a microphone. I didn't feel safe in my own home. I lay awake at night wondering how my life had come to this. This wasn't what I had envisioned when Danny took my hand

and we walked down the church aisle as a young hopeful married couple.

The next day the same 'electricians' returned, but this time they left a card with the landscaper. The card claimed them to be investigators for Long Island Power Authority (LIPA); they asked the landscaper to have me call them. I called my attorney. He called them. A LIPA official explained to my lawyer there were reports of meter tampering and stealing electricity and LIPA investigators would need to inspect the premises. He made no mention of anyone being in my house, or in my basement for hours the day before. My lawyer called me back and suggested I give LIPA permission for them to come back, which I did. Arrangements were made for the investigators to come the following afternoon when I would be home. They arrived with cameras and a clipboard full of notes. They took several pictures while they were in the basement and more pictures inside the house and of the outside meter. I did not follow them around. The heavyset investigator told me there was a dangerous illegal meter bypass, which they fixed. They would be back the next day to monitor the meter. They insisted Danny was responsible for this bypass, but no one could say or would say who was in my basement for six hours two days previous. None of this made any sense. I was suspicious of everyone and everything and was certain the detectives were out to get me. The third time the LIPA inspectors came, Danny was there with his own attorney. Danny's lawyer spoke with the investigators and said if they needed further information to contact him. The investigation was between Danny, his attorney and LIPA. I was out of the picture. As far as I knew this matter had nothing to do with me, was out of my hands and was being taken care of by Danny's attorney.

Danny found himself back in jail again in March of 2003 for another DWI he got while living in East Hampton the summer before. While he was behind bars, it was Generosa who made the decisions regarding my alimony. I detested that she governed my finances. I reluctantly admitted that she didn't have to give me a dime; it wasn't her responsibility to support me while Danny was locked up, although in reality it was her money no matter how you looked at it. One year later all means of support came to a screeching stop.

2003

ARRESTED

"You gain strength, courage and confidence by every experience in which you really stop to look fear in the face. You are able to say to yourself, I have lived through this horror. I can take the next thing that comes along. You must do the thing you think you cannot do."
~ Eleanor Roosevelt

Danny had a new wife for over a year but still thought of me as his possession, to which I achieved my sick little glory. When he was in jail, he'd call *me* up. He'd shout orders, expecting me to jump when he snapped his fingers. Usually, I did, but not without a yelling match. The only way I knew how to assert myself was to yell louder than him. We had been at each other's throats for several days because Little Dan wanted to quit school. He had just turned seventeen and did not need my permission. I was at my wit's end and ready to give in. Dan and I had battled on the phone early in the morning of Friday, April 4, 2003. He screamed at me that I was a bad mother for letting my child quit and I screamed back that it wasn't easy raising three kids on my own. I slammed the phone down, grabbed my car keys and headed to work cursing at myself for letting him get to me. I was driving along on the Long Island Expressway preoccupied in my thoughts wondering how I was going to get my son to stay in school; a former A-student, yet failing in every subject. I knew he was rebelling over everything that had happened. Leaving school was his way to lash back. I was frightened he'd take the alcohol-drug route so many kids did under lesser circumstances. He was genuinely a good kid. I never had any problems with him. I felt guilty that I would let him quit. Danny's words rang in my ear. It was my fault. I was a failure as a mother. I pushed those thoughts from my mind and focused on more pleasant things – like leaving work early that day to attend a retreat with Carol at the lovely little church she and I had started to attend at the beginning of the year. From the very first Sunday, I knew this was the place for me. Even though I don't think of myself as a religious person, at least not in the traditional sense of religion, I immediately felt uplifted by Pastor Lydia's real-life approach to her sermons that always seemed to relate to my life.

Thinking about what a great weekend I was going to have surrounded by loving individuals, I looked up to see a cop behind me with his light on; I pulled over. I realized I didn't have my seat belt on. The cop swaggered over to my car, glared in at me with ice-blue eyes and recited the official memorized spiel. I handed over my papers and asked what I did wrong, irritated by the interruption. He informed me that I had failed to signal when I changed lanes. I hadn't given much thought to what he had said at that moment but realized later, I *hadn't* changed lanes. I was still in the right lane having just gotten onto the LIE from Exit 68. He told me to step out of the car and stand behind it. I had never heard of doing that. I only had one other minor traffic violation in my life and was not asked to get out of my car. I was leery and not sure of what to do. But I did as I was told. He ran my license to check for warrants while we were standing outside. He towered over me and radioed to headquarters with one of those walk-talkie contraptions they wear on their shirt. Within seconds a report was back - there *was* a warrant out for my arrest! I assured him this had to be a mistake. I wanted to know what the warrant was for. The cop talked with his jaw shut, calling me 'Ma'm' and told me he was taking me to the precinct. My stomach went into a spasm. The minor irritation I felt earlier escalated into major fear. I attempted to explain to him that there must be confusion with my insurance company. I had switched from one company to another and the motor vehicle department had notified me that my auto insurance had lapsed. I had immediately gone to the DMV and had the matter taken care of and received the proper documents stating this fact, which were in the console of my car. The police officer would not let me get them. He repeated in that locked-jaw gruff voice that he did not know what the warrant was for, but that I was under arrest. He pulled my arms behind my back and snapped the cuffs on. He would not hear me out or allow me the chance to retrieve the papers. I pleaded with him to let me drive my car to the precinct. Instead, he shoved me in the back of the police car, like a dog. I feared I was going to be raped, or worse. I knew there was no warrant for me. And there was no way out of that car. I was handcuffed in the back of a police car, powerless. Being taken somewhere I did not believe to be the police department. I had recently seen a TV talk show about women who were raped by police officers, or men who pretend to be officers, the show emphasized they never get to the second location. I cried silent salty tears that trickled down my cheeks and dropped onto my blouse. I could not believe this was happening.

The officer's cold blue eyes peered at me from the rearview mirror, he seemed to find pleasure in my terror. Fight or flight. My old psychology courses came to mind. For a fraction of a second, the body freezes in motion. Shuts down. Shock. Immobilized. Fear so great, it's paralyzing. Pupils dilate. Muscles tighten, ready for action. Adrenals kick in. Rapid short breaths. I was experiencing all of them.

We arrived at the Seventh Precinct on William Floyd Parkway in Shirley. I was relieved that I wasn't taken to some deserted wooded area. I was at a police station and trusted someone there would help me. But help was not coming then or at all. I was yanked from the car, pulled by my arm and escorted to a back door into a windowless 8 x 8 cinder block concrete cubicle. It was not an overactive imagination or too much television that convinced me I was about to be raped on the cold cement floor where no one would hear my screams. In fact, I believed that other officers would one by one violate me and they would all get away with it. Why wouldn't my mind go in that direction? I knew I had no warrants out on me. Frightening, unbelievable events had already taken place in my life.

Gratefully, I was not raped. I was told to sit in the chair. The cop menacingly joked that he was going to shackle me to the floor. I pleaded like the captive that I was. Crying, blubbering. I wiped snot on my blouse. I begged him to let me use my phone. I needed to call my job. I knew everyone would be worried about me. This tall cop with silver hair and icy blue eyes had a moment of compassion. He assured me he would notify my job, went so far as to take the phone number down. As he walked out of the room, he turned back to look at me, in a kind voice he told me not to worry. He said he would try to find out what the warrant was for. I was left alone, my hands cuffed behind my back, sitting under a glaring fluorescent light. I prayed.

I don't know how long the officer was gone, maybe fifteen to twenty minutes. I jumped when I heard the door open. He asked me if I ever left a restaurant without paying a bill. I had no idea what he was talking about. The warrant was for Theft of Services. He said maybe it was an accident, that I left a restaurant without realizing I didn't pay. He was being suspiciously nice. Thoughts raced through my mind trying to recall when I had been out to dinner and who I was with. Usually, we would split the tab evenly. Even if there were the remote chance that one of us forgot to pay the bill, how would they have gotten my name? Did that mean that whoever I had dinner with had a warrant out as well? This was beyond bizarre.

The police officer looked as confused as I was. He left again saying he'd find out what was going on. All of a sudden, he was my buddy!

Not ten minutes later he was back; the warrant was from LIPA. I sighed a breath of relief. Now I knew this was a misunderstanding. Attorneys were handling the case; all I needed to do was give the officer the lawyer's phone number and the matter would be resolved. But he left again before I had the chance to explain this to him.

The door opened again, but it wasn't the mean-officer-turned-nice-officer, it was the two homicide detectives who just happened to be at this particular precinct at the same time I was there, the same two detectives who had previously been informed that my attorney would need to be present if they wished to question me. But I had forgotten about the verbal agreement and never thought to ask for my lawyer. They sat their suited bodies across the table from me not caring I was handcuffed like a convict. They briefly flashed a legal-looking paper before me that stated "LIPA Against Pelosi." I have no idea whether it said Tamara Pelosi or not.

The older stocky detective pointed his thick stubby finger at the document. Not caring that he was basically bribing me he told me this was a felony; if I want a-get-out-of-jail-free-card, I should give them the info they want. But I told them as I had numerous times before, that I knew nothing, I wasn't even sure exactly when Mr. Ammon was murdered. The same detective, with obvious years of badgering and terrifying people, slammed his fat fist on the desk. He yelled so loud "on your fucking son Anthony's birthday," that foamy spit flew across the room like a rabid dog. I was stunned by the rage of this man in a gray suit and tie. While the rageful older one yelled at me, called me names and accused me of withholding information, the younger slimmer one spoke in a soft voice, suggested it would be best if I cooperated, otherwise I could spend a long time in jail. All I wanted was to call my daughter and tell her I was safe. The *good-cop* said he would check with the arresting officer if a call had been made to my job. Two minutes later he was back with a phone in his hand. No one had called. He placed the phone on the table, plugged it in an outlet, mercifully removed the cuffs, and leaned his face over mine, close enough that I could smell coffee on his breath. No longer the *good cop*, he threatened if I knew what was good for me, I wouldn't let on that I was in the middle of an interrogation. He wanted me to lie and say there was a mix-up with my license and I'd call back when I had the chance.

Amazingly I remembered my work number. Although I desperately wanted to scream for help when Carol answered the phone, I managed to compose myself and recite the instructed script I was given. Carol wanted to come to the precinct, but I quickly hung up telling her I would call her later. I knew Carol would not idly sit and wait for me to call her back. I found out much later that day she had immediately called my mother and the two of them set off on a quest to find me and solve the mystery.

I was interrogated for several hours; grilled and drilled endlessly on the same questions I had already answered dozens of times at my house. These two men who dressed so meticulously in business suits they could have been bankers, browbeat me, intimated me and threatened me; they told me they could put me in jail and basically throw away the key. They boasted they had clout, if I knew what was good for me, I'd open my mouth and spill the beans. If I gave them what they wanted they had the power to drop the Theft of Service charges. They played games with my head, from bullying me to pacifying me, to bragging what nice guys they were, so nice they would drop the felony charge to a misdemeanor. Their goal was to wear me down and they did, but not in the way they hoped. I finally told them I had nothing more to say to them. They could go ahead and charge me with the felony and put me in jail, I was too emotionally and mentally exhausted to care. My depressed mental state did not influence the detectives. They joked back and forth between each other on what they could do with my charges, they settled on a misdemeanor. They informed me they would be transporting me from the Seventh Precinct to the Fifth Precinct in another town, where supposedly the charges would be processed. This made no sense to me, but nothing that had taken place that morning made any sense. Handcuffs once again were locked tight around my wrists, formalities they said. I was escorted to an unmarked car, with a detective on either side of me holding on to my arms as if I was going to make a mad dash to freedom.

Squinting from the bright sun after being closed in the dungeon for what must have been hours, (I had no conception of time), I spotted both my mother's and Carol's cars in the parking lot. I told the detectives I needed to go back inside since my mother and Carol must have been there waiting for me, but they continued to usher me to their car, mumbling that my mother and Carol had only arrived a few moments before and would be meeting me at the Fifth Precinct to bail me out, which was the first I heard of being bailed out. I could not understand how they knew about my mother and Carol but was too exhausted to ask. I was more baffled than before. This was like trying to put a thousand-piece jigsaw puzzle together with half the pieces missing. There was no logical reasoning for anything. None at all. What I learned later was that Carol and my mother had been at the Seventh Precinct for over an hour getting the run-a-round from the police. They were told conflicting stories, first that I was not there, then no one seemed to know what precinct I was at. At some point, while I was left alone, the two detectives questioned my mother for about half an hour. They strongly suggested my mother encourage me to cooperate with them, otherwise, her daughter was facing a felony charge. Neither my mother nor Carol knew I was there the same time as they were; they were told I was at another station. In the meantime, my mother contacted my attorney who had also been given the run-a-round from the police. He called several police stations before anyone admitted where I was and had the chance to speak with me. I was transported to the Fifth Precinct station in the backseat of an unmarked car, and taken in handcuffs to a side door of the building. The detectives led me down a bleak gray hallway. To the right of the hallway were dark, almost black-looking cells and to the left were tables with glass dividers for criminals. The room began to whirl, the dismal grays and blacks spun before my eyes, my knees gave way and I slumped to the floor. The terrifying reality of the sinister-looking cells and the frightening interrogation room brought on a full-blown panic attack. I began to hyperventilate and was not able to breathe, sharp pains stabbed my chest. I had had other attacks before, but nothing compared to this. The detectives helped me to my feet, removed the cuffs and brought me a cup of water. Each detective held me under an arm and walked me to the table. I pleaded and begged for them to understand that I hadn't done anything wrong. I was not a criminal. My chest tightened to the point that I needed to gasp for air. One of the men brought the cup of water to my lips. In a low voice, the younger detective spoke to me as if I were a child or mentally disabled. He told me they were almost done, but I still needed to be fingerprinted. He evidently caught the terror in my eyes, and in a rather kind tone explained it was part of the procedure. I was taken to the area where the fingerprinting was set up in the back part of the building. The officer grabbed one finger at a time, rolled it on an ink pad and pressed each finger on some sort of machine. My hand shook so much it annoyed the policeman who had to go through the procedure several times to get a decent print. After that degrading experience came a more shameful one - the mug shot. I was ordered to place my feet on top of the shoe prints that were painted on the floor and look into the camera. A flash went off. My mug shot was on record. When they were finished putting me through this mortifying ordeal, I was brought back to the interrogation room. I was informed I would be released in a few minutes once some paperwork was completed. A phone was handed to me that appeared from nowhere; it was my attorney. After a quick inquiry about how I was doing, he gave me a brief encapsulation of what it took for him to finally locate me. He advised me not to speak to anyone until he got there, but since I had already been telling the detectives everything I knew and believed I was about to be released I told my attorney it wasn't necessary for him to come. I would be out before he could get there. I promised to call him as soon as I could.

For a few moments, I was alone. I don't think I was ever as exhausted as I was then. With my head on my arms on top of the table, I sobbed quietly. My body began to tremble uncontrollably, more from nerves than cold, but someone did bring me my jacket. I urgently needed to use the restroom. I thought I could wait until I was released, which I believed was any minute. But after another half an hour of sitting at the table, nature was screaming, I couldn't contain my bladder a moment longer. A female officer escorted me to the ladies' room and stood in there with me. When I came out of the stall, she told me she would need to search me. I was directed to lower my pants. I thought I was going to faint. Thankfully there was a knock on the door informing the police officer I was being released. I was never searched. It took another half an hour to finish the processing. I bailed myself out for $50 cash. I was given a desk appearance ticket to appear in court on May 23, 2003. I had no idea what my charges were for. I don't know what I looked like, but after seven tormenting hours of emotional and mental badgering, by the expression on Carol's and my mother's face, who had been waiting for me the entire time, I was not a pleasant sight. The two of them embraced me, all three of us in tears. They bombarded me with questions, but I desperately needed to get outside and breathe some fresh air. Carol and my mother guided me out the door as if I was an invalid. With each of them supporting me we walked to Carol's car, which was parked next to mine. I asked them how my car got there. Of course, they had no idea. The three of us looked at one another, another puzzle piece missing. It was never clear how my car got from the Long Island Expressway where I was handcuffed and forced into the police car. I had been under the impression that when someone was arrested their vehicle was towed away, or left where it was. It was also a mystery why my mother, Carol and my attorney were given such a run-around.

My kids nearly bowled me over when I walked in the door. Rachelle knew something serious had happened when I didn't show up for work, but it wasn't until much later in the day, after Carol and my mother located me at the police station, that she learned of the arrest. She and Little Dan had been extremely worried, Tony was quiet and withdrawn. All three huddled around me on the couch asking questions I couldn't answer. How could I explain what had taken place when I myself was mystified? When I finally got to speak with my attorney, he was outraged by what was done to me. He had spoken with a representative from LIPA who knew nothing of a warrant or of any charges against me. He encouraged me to file a lawsuit, as well as a civil suit. A few days after I was arrested, I learned that my arrest was apparently a complicated 'sting' that was carefully executed. Within the next twenty-four hours, three of Danny's friends and his cousin were pulled over by unmarked cars while on their way to work, hauled to the police station and interrogated for hours regarding the murder of Mr. Ammon. I was their first target and the only one arrested on the pretense of a false charge.

2003

HUMILIATION

"May the Lord give you peace."
~ The Greeting of St. Francis of Assisi

Eight hours after I was yanked from my car, handcuffed and carted off to the police station, Carol was back at my house encouraging me to attend our women's weekend retreat that I had been looking forward to that morning. But I was too emotionally drained to move myself off the couch and pack a few things and I didn't want to leave my kids – or my home for that matter. But both Carol and my mother convinced me that a weekend of rest was what I needed. While I was in the shower my mother threw some clothes together in an overnight bag and reassured me my kids would be under her care. I had originally planned to take my car, but both Carol and I were suspicious the police had 'bugged' my car, so we decided to use Carol's. If the car had been wired, all they would have heard was me sobbing. I cried the entire weekend. My eyes were swollen little slits; my voice was hoarse. No one but Carol knew what had happened. By the end of the second day, I found the courage to speak with Pastor Lydia. I told her about my life and what led up to the arrest. She held my hands and prayed over me. Instantly a calming sensation penetrated every cell. The tension in my face and jaw slipped away. My shoulders relaxed. There was a sense of peace that I couldn't get with Xanax. Pastor Lydia told me a story about how Jesus had to rise above his pain. She vowed that one-day God was going to use this experience in a way I could never imagine. She suggested I pray for Danny; pray that he could find peace in his life. She explained the importance of forgiving him in order for me to go on with my life. I cried healing tears throughout the weekend until there were no tears left to cry. I was grateful for the two days away and for Pastor Lydia's compassionate words of wisdom. I was actually able to smile by the time the retreat was over on Sunday afternoon.

Heading to work Monday morning, feeling a sense of calm, I received a call from Tony's school guidance counselor. She told me she had tried to contact me several times on Friday to let me know Tony had a 'melt down' while in school. For no apparent reason that she knew of, he started to cry in the classroom and was sent to her office where he continued to cry non-stop for hours. When she asked him what was wrong he answered he didn't know, but could not stop crying. Eventually, his tears subsided and she allowed him to take the bus home. When I learned of my son's distress, I was furious with the detectives who kept me locked away at the police station while my son needed me and guilty that I had gone away for the weekend unaware of the pain my young son was experiencing. I was so enmeshed in my own misery I never noticed how troubled he was. My mother reported he was sad and gloomy over the weekend, but she attributed his quietness to my arrest and my being away; he never mentioned anything to her or to me when I returned home Sunday night.

According to the counselor Tony was sent to her office at ten-thirty and calmed down around two; around the same hours, I was being harassed. Coincidence? I don't think so. Tony may not know what made him so upset on that Friday on April 4, 2003, but I have no doubt my son picked up on my distress.

I had taken my attorney's advice and was going ahead with the civil suit. He had recommended a young lawyer who would represent the five of us who had been taken in for questioning. Unbeknown to me, the lawyer decided to hold a press conference. The media went into a crazed frenzy when they learned that my name was part of the suit. Somehow the reporters discovered where I worked and raided my job like a pack of famished canines. A half dozen or more news people arrived on the property of my center within half an hour from the press conference, unfortunately at the exact time parents were picking their children up. The reporters grabbed every parent they could and gorged on each bit of information they could get their teeth into. They brazenly knocked on the center's door looking for me. I hid upstairs in my office wishing I could crawl in a hole for the rest of my life. The Program Director told them I was unavailable for comments and asked them to leave. They lingered after all the children were gone. Eventually, they got the message and vacated the grounds in the same rushed mania they arrived in. Carol sat with me for a while to be sure I was all right to drive home. We discussed what this incident might do to our center. We thought it best to immediately send letters to the parents explaining what had taken place, rather than waiting for them to read a distorted version in the newspapers. I decided to take two weeks off work for things to calm down. I did not want to put the school or the center in jeopardy. Driving home in a stupefied daze I wondered what the parents would think of me. I was prepared for parents to sign their children out of the school. After all, who would want their child to be around a *criminal?* As I turned into my road, I saw reporters gathered in front of my house, I made a quick U-turn and headed to my mothers', my stomach locked in cramps.

Carol called me over the next several days reporting the outpouring of letters that came to the center, letters from the parents expressing their support, how much they admired me not just as a teacher, but as an individual. Many sent personal handwritten notes offering words of encouragement along with bouquets of flowers and thoughtful gifts. I was overwhelmed and deeply touched by their response. But no acts of genuine kindness could eradicate my embarrassment.

On Friday, May 23, 2003, the date of my first court appearance, I was terrified I was going to be convicted for a Theft of Services charge, simply stated—stealing electricity. I spent the night curled in a fetal position with horrific stomach pains and a pounding vice-like headache. By the time morning arrived, I was weak and debilitated. My friend Patti, who is a court advocate for women, came with me for support. There was some confusion when we got there. My name wasn't on the court calendar, there was no docket number, nor proof of warrant for my arrest, yet I needed to appear before the judge. My attorney felt certain the case would be dismissed that day, but to his surprise, it moved forward regardless. The motion to dismiss was denied. I was informed I would have to face a jury of my peers and plead not guilty. That was it. Two days of stress, two hours of court, and another court date for June 21. My lawyer did his best to reassure me that the matter would be dropped once the judge read the thick folder he had prepared in my defense. However, this drama went on for two years, every month a court date, every month a postponement. Every month I'd be sick for days prior to court. No one seemed to know what was going on, except I was told to be prepared for a week-long trial. My attorney decided not to represent me since he was going to be one of my witnesses, so another lawyer took over. Each time I appeared before the Judge it was the same humiliation I had experienced on the day I was arrested. I was obsessed with shame. No matter how much I primed myself emotionally and mentally, no matter who came with me, no matter what the attorneys believed, I was petrified. Ironically, a warrant for my arrest was never produced, yet every month I had to appear in court for the Theft of Service charge, only to have each appearance postponed.

Two weeks after my arrest, right after Easter, Little Dan quit school. He simply didn't return after vacation. He had no interest in anything and my arrest didn't help matters. His escape was to hang out with his friends; they were his safety net. I couldn't argue with him, I knew how he felt. If I didn't have to support my family, I would have quit my job and buried my head under my pillows.

I had a lot on my plate; in fact, it was so overloaded I could barely distinguish one day from the other; one calamity from another. There were rumors that the prosecution had called for a Grand Jury to gather sufficient evidence to arrest Danny for the murder of Mr. Ammon. The grand jury was scheduled to begin sometime in July. There was some speculation as to whether my name was on the list, as it turned out it was. The District Attorney called my attorney who notified me. This new and alarming information was up on the *Top Ten Things I Do Not Need In My Life, Now Or Ever*. I was already ravaged with anxiety over my own trial and now a Grand Jury as a witness *against* Danny! If I were a drug addict I would have zoned out on some mind-altering narcotic. Instead, I delved deeper into my church, attended as many inspirational workshops that I could and entrusted my life in God's hands.

After a long, hard hot day at work, I was grateful for a cool shower and a relaxing evening. The kids were out and about doing what kids do on summer evenings. The house was blissfully quiet in comparison to the energetic exuberance of fifty little kids at summer camp. Feeling content and peaceful I sat down to eat a light dinner and browse through the *Suffolk Life*, a local newspaper. A story about the Guide Dog Foundation on the front page caught my interest. I placed one forkful of food in my mouth, turned to the page where the story continued and across from the picture of a Golden Retriever puppy was my *mug shot*! Along with Danny's and some strangers and a lengthy article of the LIPA investigation and the Long Islanders who were arrested for *stealing* electricity. *My* face and *my* name in connection with these total strangers for all *Suffolk Life* subscribers to read, including the parents whose children attended my center! I leaped from the table, knocked the chair over and coughed up a piece of lettuce I had gasped down my throat. My fingers zipped across the phone buttons dialing my attorney and left a message on his machine. Then I called Danny's attorney who was handling his LIPA case. I wailed to him, '*how did THAT picture get in the newspaper?*' He responded in a mechanical, not very sympathetic tone, something about free press, nothing he could do, it was within the law for my mug shot to be printed. I spent my days tucked away in my office, far from the pitying glares, too ashamed to see anyone. I refused to participate in the kids' programs for fear a parent might see me. Two days after my public condemnation my lawyer called me; I was due to appear before the Grand Jury on Monday, July 14. I was at the Riverhead Courthouse with my mother by nine Monday morning after a long fretful sleepless weekend. I've learned over the years if you want to present a confident persona, dress in a manner to support the illusion. With my blonde hair neatly pulled up and back with a clasp and a tan business suit, one would have thought *I* was the one to boldly defend some unfortunate soul. Instead, I was the unfortunate soul. Appearing before a Grand Jury is unlike anything I have ever experienced. I was seated in a hard-backed chair, which was almost in the middle of the room, surrounded in a horseshoe shape by thirty or so jurors. There is no judge or legal representation at a grand jury. You are on your own with thirty pairs of unrelenting eyes glued to you. The DA sat at a rectangular table to the right of me, accompanied by her assistant who continuously shuffled through a stack of folders laden with a copious supply of investigative materials. I learned in a matter of minutes not to be fooled by the diminutive size of the slightly built District Attorney; after all a stick of dynamite is not very large. After the prefatory swearing-in, the DA hammered away posing the same questions as the homicide detectives, "Did Danny give me a stun gun? Why did Danny give me a stun gun? Where was Danny on the night of the murder? What was Danny wearing when he came over to my house on Sunday morning October 21, 2001? How was he behaving? Do I know where the missing hard drive is? Did Danny deposit huge amounts of money in my personal bank accounts? Did Danny ever admit to me that he murdered Mr. Ammon?"

As per my attorney, I answered only what was asked; I followed his instruction even though I wanted to explain why I said what I did. Occasionally I caught a few jurors nodding their heads in agreement or maybe in understanding. But one juror, in particular, a gray-haired older woman in her sixties or so, rolled her eyes up as if she couldn't be bothered listening to me, as though she believed I was lying. I am convinced it was no accident my mug shot was displayed for open criticism five days before I was to stand in front of a grand jury. For brief moments the interrogation subsided as the DA and her assistant sorted through their myriad of papers. Then as if they hadn't heard a word I said, parroted the same questions. On and on and on for an hour and a half.

I had hoped that I had hoodwinked the jurors and perhaps the DA as well, by masquerading as a secure undaunted witness. Obviously not. One month later on the thirteenth of August, I was again called to the grand jury. Dressed in yet another business suit, a crème-colored silk scarf around my neck clasped to my suit with a delicate gold Angel pin and my hair falling loose, whatever false bravado I may have exhibited the last time, was flushed down the toilet with my breakfast. For the District Attorney to want me back could only mean one of two things, either I said something important enough worth repeating or this DA planned to abuse and denounce my statements in the hope of bringing me to my knees and spilling forth whatever the prosecution needed to seal their case against Danny. A half an hour into the interrogation with the DA repeating the queries she had asked for over an hour four weeks ago, and which were harped on repeatedly over the course of a year by the homicide detectives, I came to doubt if I had divulged anything new or of substantial significance. And since I was *not* concealing any information, she diligently pressed on. I became agitated by the monotonous repetitious rhetoric, which if nothing else, dispelled my fear. I wanted to lash out at *her*, question *her*, 'who issued my arrest? *Who* manipulated my mug shot to appear in a widely read newspaper quite *coincidentally* a few days prior to my appearance at the grand jury? The diatribe continued for another hour. Whether I provided the prosecution with anything different than the last time, I didn't know, but

mercifully, I was not requested to appear before the Grand
Jury again. However, the Grand Jury resumed for some
months to come, collecting evidence and ample testimony for
Danny's intended arrest. I kept the kids away from their father
as much as possible. No one could ascertain when the time
would come when he would be apprehended and under what
conditions; it could happen at a family evening gathering.
Whatever or however the arrest would take place, my kids did
not need to witness their father being handcuffed and
roughshod away by a swarm of broad-shouldered men in
business suits.

Every day the newspapers, both local and national, reported
some story regarding "The East Hampton Murder" and
whatever current situation there was. The new headline that
grabbed the interest of the masses in August of 2003 wasn't
about the murder per se, but about Generosa – *"Ammon Widow
Dies of Cancer"*. I had heard a rumor that Generosa had been
diagnosed with breast cancer some months before, but in all
honesty, I thought it was one of Danny's stories. Even when he
told our children that Generosa had made him move out
because she didn't want him seeing her deteriorate; I still
thought it sounded a bit too dramatic to be true. But on
August 25, Generosa succumbed to the disease, taking with
her the possible link to who murdered her former husband. To
my children, her death meant freedom for their father. They,
in their innocence, blamed Generosa for taking their father
and keeping him away. I understood their happiness to have
their father back in their lives but brought to their attention
that two young children were now without a father and a
mother. My heart went out to the twins who had become close
step-siblings to Tony. The following day on the cover of the
New York Post was a picture of Danny sitting bleary-eyed at the
Stanhope Hotel's lounge with a cigarette dangling from his

lips, a drink in front of him, and a shopping bag with Generosa's ashes sitting on top of the bar. Next to her ashes were her favorite drink and a lit cigarette burning in an ashtray for her. The story titled, "To You, Generosa – Pelosi Toasts Ashes of Wife in Bar Where They Met." The story described how Danny snatched Generosa's ashes from the funeral home and how, at her request, wanted Danny to have a drink for them after her death in memory of when they first met. All I could do was shake my head in disgust.

2004

GLORY AND GRIEF

"Whatever hour God has blessed you with, take it with a grateful hand."
~ Horace

I took a break from the daily 'Danny headlines' and flew down to Melbourne in September to celebrate my fortieth birthday with my zany pal Joy and her jaunty fire department buddies that she worked with. These compassionate and courageous men whose job it is to save lives, helped in saving mine. They sent me home with an overdose of a super-duper laughter strong enough to last a good long while.

In the meantime, while I was away, my mother and Rachelle planned a surprise fortieth birthday party for me. In less than a week, they managed to put together a gathering of twenty-five of my dearest female friends. My mother asked if each one of the girls would give a little speech on why they chose to celebrate my birthday with me. Halfway through the tributes, all the women were bawling! My mother wrote me two poems and saved them to the end. The first one was a comical litany on how we differed as mother and daughter and the second a reflection of my life from birth to present day as seen through her eyes. Twenty-five emotional, peri-menopausal women gathered in one room could be a dangerous thing! In between tears, there were giggles, from silent sobs to hearty guffaws, screeches and screams. Laughter really is the best medicine. I am grateful for these interludes of mirth that replenished my soul and helped to soften my facial muscles that had begun to take on the appearance of a chiseled face of stone etched with a permanent scowl.

A miracle of sorts took place at the beginning of the school year, Little Dan decided on his own to return to school. I met with the guidance counselor and the administration to determine what options he would have and if he could graduate with his class as scheduled. The high school counselor put a program together for my oldest son. She arranged for him to double up on his classes, combining what he missed the previous year with the necessary credits for his senior year. He was only lacking a few credits and since he was an intelligent being and maintained high grades in the past, she felt confident he could pull this off with a little effort and motivation on his part. It was a glorifying feeling to have my son back in school, but it required much effort on my part to get him up in the morning. It was psychologically exhausting keeping him propelled in the direction of graduation. On the other hand, I received a letter from Tony's school stating he wasn't able to focus in the classroom due to his high anxiety and was advised he was a candidate for home tutoring. Tony was released from the public school system for the remainder of the year and put-on anti-anxiety medication. The tutoring solved the school's dilemma, but it added to my stress. I had to schedule the tutoring when an adult was home, which meant adjusting and readjusting my schedule and any other adult who could volunteer their time. Tony may have been relieved not to face the pressures of school, but he didn't relish home tutoring either. He bucked me every step of the way. In his own words, he said he felt like a 'freak.' He was already singled out as the kid whose father was thought of as a murderer. Home tutoring set him further apart from his peers.

The morning struggles with my sons continued. I didn't have to wake Tony up for school, but I was subjected to his daily protests and refusals to cooperate. This was the on-going scene in my home every day, compounded with the chore of getting his older brother Dan out of bed. I had one son who was emotionally incapable of attending school, another son who was indifferent about graduating, and a twenty-one-year-old daughter who was attempting to live a normal life. By the time I arrived at work I was an exhausted bundle of nerves.

It didn't help matters any when the holidays rolled around to have Danny show up on Christmas Eve bearing ostentatious gifts. He bought Tony an adult-sized high-priced CR125 Honda dirt bike, Rachelle enough cash for the cruise she was planning with her friends and dazzled Little Dan with a Christmas stocking filled with one thousand one-dollar bills.

I had been contemplating whether or not to resume my education. With everything that was going on in my life I didn't see how I could manage more stress. But I had discovered that delving into my studies was therapy for me; it kept my mind off of the daily pressures and what I couldn't control. My books were my salvation. I had applied for the Doctorate Program in Education and was accepted in January. It was a good way to begin the year, something positive to look forward to.

March was another story. It is the month of the Spring Equinox, it can either come in as a lamb and out like a lion or in like a lion and out like a lamb. This spring was the latter, only the lion never left, and I don't mean the weather. It was the month of dichotomies from extreme highs to irreversible lows. A month of pride. A month of grief. A month of facing realities.

Into the third week of March, Carol, (who was also working on her Doctorate), and I needed to fly down south to the university for a few days for our doctorate orientation. When we had done this in the past for our Master's, it was an exciting and exhilarating experience. We had behaved like giggling nervous schoolgirls on our first day and left feeling a sense of determination and pride, giving ourselves a big pat on our backs for our courage and fortitude. This trip, however, was anything but exhilarating. The day I left for Florida, March 17, 2004, Danny phoned me to say there were rumors of his indictment, which could be as soon as the next day. For over a year I had anguished over this day, worried about how my kids would handle their father in jail for murder. I was going to be a thousand miles away and felt powerless. I knew I could count on my mother to help them cope, but felt I should be there. But since it was a rumor and not a fact, I had to sit back and wait on pins and needles for the next phone call. I half-listened to the professor giving the doctorate students the rundown of what it was going to take to obtain their degree.

The following day, Thursday, March 18, Danny and his attorneys, accompanied by an entourage of reporters and cameramen, showed up at the Riverhead Courthouse with the understanding an indictment would be issued. Danny's lawyers thought it best that he turn himself in, rather than take the risk of a surprise arrest. But when they arrived at the courthouse no one seemed to know anything about an indictment and Danny was sent home a public spectacle. I spent the night on the phone with Rachelle and my mother keeping me posted of the outlandish events feeling completely helpless.

I was back home by Saturday, happy about the prospect of my doctorate and concerned over the mystery of Danny's indictment. It was a frustrating and bewildering dilemma with no explanation. Every day we'd wake wondering if this could be the day. Not that I wanted to see him put in jail for murder, but the suspense was taking its toll on my family. Whatever the reason for the lack of an indictment on Thursday the eighteenth, by Tuesday, March twenty-third, one was issued. The morning before Danny was to turn himself over to the authorities, he came over to the house to say goodbye to the kids. I said a quick emotional farewell and left him alone with them. He took each one privately on the side and told them he loved them that he was innocent and one day he would be able to prove it. The four of us watched him leave from my bedroom window. I kept the kids home from school. Danny was indicted one hour later for a second-degree murder charge without the former fanfare and the ballyhoo of the week before. He was handcuffed and escorted to the Riverhead jail where he was held without bail. As far as Danny was concerned, this was not a supine, pusillanimous surrender, but a statement of his innocence. He gave a brief, but exhorting speech to the press expressing his itchiness for his trial to begin and his confidence in the outcome.

In contrast to Danny's cockiness and self-assuredness, I was frightened at how brute reality was sinking in, like quicksand that sucks you deeper and deeper into the earth. I was witness to the DA's canniness; she would not be a shrinking violet to Danny's bumptious big-league attorneys.

In the middle of Danny's on again off again publicized indictment, my center held their Parent-Teacher conferences. I had no choice but to meet with the parents; escaping to my office was not an option. I often felt like I led two lives. On cue, I could snap a finger and like a genie could magically transform from a frightened, humiliated, embarrassed woman, to the professional competent co-founder and director of a private non-for-profit preschool; shame and fear kept neatly tucked away behind a forced and simulated smile.

2004

ANGELS IN ACTION

"The eye which I see God is the same eye which God sees me."
~ Meister Eckehart

Three days after Danny's indictment, Carol and one of her friends picked me up on Friday afternoon for a weekend women's retreat with Pastor Lydia. The weekend with the women from my church was just what I needed to help me sort through my emotions that were on overload, see-sawing up and down, juggled back and forth and spun round and round until I couldn't identify what I was feeling. Part of me was sad for Danny, saddened by the choices and decisions he made in his life, but a bigger part was furious with him *because* of those choices and decisions. My heart ached for my children and their innocence. They loved their father and believed *he* was the victim of this mess. We stopped at a local pizza parlor for a late lunch, but I didn't think I could eat. While they were ordering a slice of pizza and soda, I looked down at the newspapers in the stand. Glaring up at me was Danny's picture on the front page. In large bold letters it read:

ELECTRICIAN INDICTED FOR MURDER OF
WEALTHY FINANCIER

There was no escape from the fact that the man I was married to for twenty years would be on trial for murder. No snap of the finger could alter my overwhelming sadness or lessen my shameful feelings. By the time we got to the retreat, I was wishing I were home in my cocoon. Thankfully I wasn't.

The three of us shared a suite at a beautiful resort on the tip of Long Island. We dropped off our things and met Pastor Lydia and the other women at the restaurant for the orientation. The lively chatter of a hundred or so women filled the large room that was set with a dozen round tables. The three of us made our way over to an empty table and were joined by five jolly sprightly women that I recognized from church. It was immediately apparent these jovial women, all around my age, were close friends who had that special bond women have when supporting one another through hard times. Smiles went around the table and heads nodded in recollection of seeing one another at church. Pastor Lydia called the women together and asked everyone to find a seat. She opened the evening with prayers, a short sermon and a few moments of quiet reflection. Except for an occasional cough, the room was quiet. The pastor gave a brief synopsis of the weekend activities; we were to meet back at the restaurant the next morning by eight o'clock for breakfast. After breakfast, we were to divide into groups of eight, return to the resort and gather in one of the women's suite. Before leaving the restaurant that evening, we needed to discuss among us whose room we would use for our workshop. Since the five of them were friends and had been on Pastor Lydia's retreats in the past, we left the decision up to them. There didn't seem to be any question between them that we'd congregate at their suite. After light refreshments of coffee, tea and cookies, we went back to our rooms. I was relieved the evening was over and happy to retreat to the sanctity of my room. It had been a long emotional day. We were up with the roosters and ready for breakfast. My stomach was growling. I hadn't eaten anything substantial for two days. The 'happy five', as I dubbed them, met us at the restaurant. I don't think I have ever seen such glowing bubbly perpetually merry women; they laughed at everything. There wasn't a trace of despair in any of them.

After prayers, a hearty meal, and some further instruction from Pastor Lydia, we headed for the suite, the happy five leading the way. We formed a circle in the spacious room. The gaiety of the happy five was momentarily put aside as each woman shared their personal tragedy. One of the women spoke calmly about the death of her teenage son, killed in a car accident the year before. She spoke of the earth-shattering pain, the tremendous loneliness and the deafening stillness in her home. And her faith that helped her survive. I was last to speak. I did not want to talk about my personal life and wanted nothing more than to escape the ongoing shame I felt. Yet I was tired of pretending I was strong and capable. If this woman who endured the greatest tragedy a mother can experience, the death of a precious child, could still find the courage to rise out of bed every morning, find beauty in a sunset and joy in her garden and remain steadfast to her faith, then I could as well. I told them everything, spilling forth my entire scandalous story. For the first time, I revealed to strangers my terrifying arrest, the public shame and embarrassment, and the criminal charges against me. I paused, waiting for their response. One by one they came and embraced me. The weekend was more than I ever hoped it could be. For the first time in more months than I could recall I felt freed from the dark secrets that weighed heavy upon me. The women invited me to join their prayer group. Every

Thursday evening, I made sure I was there. It was *their* prayers, *their* constant faith, and *their* devotion to God that moved mountains in my life. Their endless courage and faith and the sense of peace that surrounded them were a continuous source of inspiration to me.

At the beginning of the New Year, Carol and I had been informed that we were hand-picked, along with ten other women, to be honored for the first annual "Women of the Year" award. We, like the other women, were offered the award in recognition of our dedication, our supreme efforts and the difference each of us made within our community. We were a diverse and varied group of ages, shapes, sizes, and colors. We ranged from the woman who devoted her life to saving the teenage druggies on the streets of New York City, to the woman who devoted her life to saving the stray and abandoned cats in Nassau County. Whatever the cause, each woman gave of their time and often their personal resources. Carol and I were acknowledged for our efforts to educate children on the prevention of drugs and alcohol abuse, for offering a number of support groups for families in crisis and because of our hard work and tenacity of not giving up when faced with adversity. The date of the function, March 30, was sandwiched in between Danny's indictment, and two days before my next court date, and on the second anniversary of Danny's brother's death. It wasn't until the day before the event that I discovered the theme of the ceremony was none other than, "The Wind Beneath My Wings." After mingling with our guests during the cocktail hour, the twelve honorees were asked to stand in a circle around the dance floor, our loving families and friends gathered behind us. Rising from below a portable floor in the center of our circle, drifted an ethereal mist and a lovely human angel. The woman was adorned with magnificent celestial white-feathered wings, in a melodious voice she sang Bette Midler's touching tune. The angel floated around the circle gazing at each woman as she sang. She lingered a second or two more when she reached me and lightly brushed my hand with hers. A roadside billboard could not have delivered a more powerful message; my *guardian angel* was undeniably watching over me.

During the last two weeks of March, I was filled to capacity with a huge lump of contrary emotions all squeezed into one average-sized human being. The exuberant high at the acceptance into a doctorate program; the depressing shameful low of Danny's indictment; the pride of being one of twelve women hand-picked for "Women of the Year" award; and the inspirational gift of the 'happy five'. *Whew!*

PLUGGED INTO ROBOT MODE

"Worry never robs tomorrow of its sorrow;
it only saps today of its strength."
~ A.J. Cronin

With Danny in jail and no Generosa to see that I received child support, I was left with the responsibility of caring for my children and carrying a home whose monthly expenses were triple my monthly income. After speaking with a financial advisor who was younger than my daughter, I was told I had no choice but to sell my home. That was not what I wanted to hear. I did not want to stress my kids out anymore. Our home was the only form of stability any of us had in our lives. I wound up making the decision to refinance, (really the only decision I had), to bide some time to figure out my life. To hold me over, I borrowed money from relatives and good friends. I detested being placed in that position. My blood still boils when I think of the mess Danny left me in.

I plugged myself into robot mode and mechanically got through the days. A dim flicker of light made its way into the darkness when Little Dan's teacher called to tell me she believed that he could graduate. He needed to take on some extra assignments to boost his grades and pass every test with an 85 or better. The teachers were confident he would pass his finals with flying colors. It was the most hope I had had for quite a long time. My women's prayer group prayed diligently for my family and in particular for Danny to graduate.

I was due back in court, where a jury was to be selected and a trial was scheduled to take place, exactly the same week as my son's finals. In fact, I was told the trial would more than likely end on the same day of Danny's graduation, Friday, June 26.

Running on remote mode, I hastily planned my son's graduation party. I wanted to have every last detail taken care of in case I was in court every day. My mother even suggested I plan a victory party along with Dan's graduation, but I was not all that confident.

My case was postponed again. I had a brief moment of relief knowing I wouldn't be facing a jury of my peers while my son was taking his finals, but panic quickly set in when I found out the next date was set for September – the same time Danny's murder trial was scheduled to begin. The thought of having the two of us on trial simultaneously terrified me. Besides what it would do to my children, I didn't think having my name on a court roster when Danny's name was making headlines would be beneficial to my case. I was worried that if the judge hadn't figured out that I was Danny's ex-wife at that point, she certainly would have by September and no good would come from that knowledge. My lawyer told me not to worry, go home and relax. He was sure he could get the judge to change the date. But I didn't go home and relax, I went home and collapsed.

There is a sun and it does come out from behind the clouds. On June 26, 2004, my son graduated from high school. Many of the graduates received honorary awards for exemplary grades and outstanding work within their school community. As far as I was concerned it was a miracle to see my son in a cap and gown. For him to reach that goal under the circumstances that he faced was more of an achievement than any award. When my son walked across the stage and was handed his high school diploma by the superintendent of schools, I think it was my family that hooted the loudest cheers in the auditorium. For a moment I detected sadness on my son's beaming smile. I know it was hard for him to turn his tassel to the other side of his cap without his father bearing witness to his momentous accomplishment. I had a small party at my house to celebrate Little Dan's graduation, nothing like the grand festivities I had for Rachelle. Danny's absence hovered over the meager gathering like a dark gloomy film.

2004 (SEPTEMBER—DECEMBER)

GUILTY—AS CHARGED

"Each man's life represents a road toward himself."
~ Hermann Hesse

It took over three weeks for the opposing attorneys to sift through over five hundred prospective jurors to narrow down to the twelve that would serve on the "Danny Pelosi Murder Trial." The final choice included nine women and three men that would one day seal Danny's fate and the fate of my children's lives. The trial was set to commence on September 27, 2004. My children felt it was their duty to be in court for their father. I would have preferred that they didn't go. I wondered what effect it would have on them to see their father for the first time in six months, in a courtroom, on trial for murder, but I allowed each one to make their own decision. I thought it best that I wasn't there. To see Danny sitting in a room accused of a brutal murder would have been more than my raw unsettled emotions could handle. I knew I would wind up feeling sorry for him, that out of all the human emotions, pity would be the one that would rise to the surface. The press had hounded me for over three years; I was sure my presence at Danny's trial would open a Pandora's Box that I preferred to keep sealed, for my children and for myself.

The burden of the trial drove a wedge deeper into my family, each of us fled to our own place of escape for as long as we could. My schoolwork was definitely a distraction, but a temporary one. At night I was alone with my own tormented thoughts, playing the gruesome murder scene over and over again in my mind. My two older children were certain their father was innocent and my youngest was too withdrawn to know what tortured thoughts he had. As for me, I didn't know anything anymore. I couldn't imagine Danny savagely beating someone to death. I did not believe it was possible. Yet I wondered.

The trial continued for three agonizing months. Everyday daunting testimonies piled up against Danny, including his own father testifying against him. Yet, even with all the forensic experts, there wasn't actual evidence or sufficient circumstantial evidence that would prove Danny was guilty. It seemed very possible that Danny would be found innocent. But on Monday morning, December 13, 2004, after the jury was sequestered for the weekend the guilty verdict came in. I will never forget that day. I had put the radio on as soon as I got to work. Staff members were hovered around the small radio waiting to hear the verdict. I felt as if I was watching a scene from an old 1940's movie, expecting to hear President Roosevelt announce the attack on Pearl Harbor. Rachelle, who worked with me, was sitting on the floor with her arms wrapped around her knees. Seven of us were glaring at the radio when the verdict was broadcast. Rachelle fell on her side, still holding her knees to her chest reeling back and forth screaming in despair that her father was not guilty. Her frail body contorted as if in a seizure. Our young Program Director scooped her up and rocked her in his strong bear-like arms. I was momentarily frozen in my spot, incapable of taking in a breath. I found out later I had screamed when the verdict came in. I called my sons at home but they hadn't heard the news. It tore my heart to have to tell them this devastating information. When Rachelle finally calmed down, we headed home chauffeured by my staff who would not let either of us drive. My mother had gotten to my house before I did. She told me she found Little Dan sitting on the loveseat staring at the TV with his girlfriend next to him. He was clicking the remote from one channel to another as if he had to hear the report from all stations to be certain there were no mistakes. Tony was lying down on the couch with a blank expression on his face; tears were quietly running down his face. When we pulled into my driveway, I took a deep breath. I knew my heart would break the moment I witnessed my children's agony, and worse, I knew I was powerless to take their suffering away.

Rachelle ran past me into the house straight to her brother Danny. When I walked in, they were in the living room, hugging and sobbing on each other, my eighteen-year-old son, not quite a man, holding his older sister up. They cried, intertwined as one broken heart, that they would never see their father again. Tony was on his bed with his arms limp alongside of him. A steady stream of silent tortured tears rolled one after the other down his innocent face. He wouldn't talk to me. I ached to hold my youngest child close to me and soothe him in my arms like a baby. But he wasn't a baby, he was a fourteen-year-old 5' 7" unapproachable non-verbal adolescent. Instead, I wiped his tears and stroked his face lightly with my fingers. I lay down next to him and placed my arm across him. Everyone left us to be with our grief. The house was quiet, except for the little whimpers escaping from Rachelle's throat. She was curled on the couch with her boyfriend sitting idly next to her, helpless of what to do. Tony stayed in his room, his TV on low. Little Dan stood outside on the porch; one tear rolled down his hairless teenage cheek. The memory of that Fourth of July so long ago flashed through my mind, my little son on top of his father's shoulders saying he was so happy water was coming from his eyes. The water coming from Little Dan's eyes this sorrowful day was anything but happy. It was as if someone had died. And in a way it was. The death of life as we knew it. A funeral without the body. The slow and painful mourning process lay before us. Before the day was over reporters were at my door begging for a statement. I pulled the drapes closed and the four of us huddled together in the living room. We attempted to resume some degree of normalcy the day after the crushing verdict. Little Dan went to work, but Rachelle, Tony and I stayed home. Tony remained in his room most of the day, emerging only to get some food or use the bathroom. Rachelle spent the time crying on the phone with one friend after another. I had to delve into a forty-page final paper and exam for my doctorate studies that was due that night and to which I only found out at six in the morning what my paper would be on. The professor had announced at the beginning of the course that the final paper would be a surprise, giving the students only twenty-four hours to complete and would count as half of the final grade.

Despite the fact that every newspaper had Danny's face sprawled across the front page with bold headlines, I could not allow myself to wallow in my family's life-altering event. A term paper was due; that was my focus. In between sorting through hundreds of pages I downloaded from the Internet and trying to assemble the information needed for my paper, I answered dozens of phone calls from friends and family and spoke to at least five or six individuals who came to my door to see how we were doing. My mother came over in the afternoon with lunch then back again later with dinner ready to give me a hand with both the paper and the well-meaning calls and visits. By ten that evening after sixteen hours of non-stop work, I forwarded my final paper to the professor. Late that night even though exhausted and bleary-eyed I read some of the stories about Danny.

"Danny Pelosi swallowed hard and buried his head in his hands when a jury delivered its verdict Monday: guilty of the second-degree murder of millionaire financier Ted Ammon…."

"A jury of nine women and three men deliberated for 23 hours over three days before deciding unanimously that Pelosi was guilty beyond a reasonable doubt of beating Ammon to death in the bedroom of his expansive East Hampton beach home on October 21, 2001……"

"The Prosecuting Attorney contends that Pelosi, who crossed himself just before the jury forewoman announced the verdict, was optimistic that he was going to get away with murder….."

"Pelosi who remains jailed without bail faces 25 years to life in prison when he is sentenced January 25……."

"Now It's His Turn To Cry," was written in bold letters across the front page of the *New York Post*.

It didn't matter how many tabloids had Danny's name and face plastered across the front page, I could not adjust to the fact that it was the man I was married to for nearly twenty years, the father of my children whom they were referring to. Who could have ever imagined that this was how our lives would end up? That night I buried my sobs in my pillow.

In the midst of the surrealistic events, my professor emailed me; I passed my final exam with a 98% and received 100% on my forty-page report. My focus on my studies was undoubtedly a therapeutic escape route.

Christmas of 2004 sorely lacked any holiday merriment. As the clock ticked to midnight, I still expected Danny to make his grand entrance with an armload of presents for everyone. My two older children made the decision to visit their father in jail over the holidays. Normally the inmates are allowed to sit with their family at a table in a large room, but Danny was on suicide watch. Instead, their visit consisted of them sitting on stools and peering into a small glass widow of a 4 X 4 block cubicle. They were shocked to see their father, not in his expensive custom-tailored suit, but wearing a drab green prison uniform, his hands cuffed in front of him with a huge lock and thick chains down to his legs shackling his ankles. Their one means of communication was through a little speaker below the window. Throughout the heart-wrenching hour, Danny sobbed to his children and begged for forgiveness. He was remorseful, as he should be. He preyed on his children's sympathies, his children who loved him unconditionally. I remember only too well how his large sad puppy eyes could melt my heart. Like some melodramatic movie of the 1950s, the three of them touched the small glass window with their fingers. Danny pleaded with his two older children to watch over their little brother and listen to their mother. But unlike actors playing a part, they wept real tears for the end of a life as they knew it. Christmas that year was not the victory Danny believed he would be celebrating, but an agonizing realistic defeat.

2005

THE COURAGE TO CHANGE THE THINGS
I CAN

" God grant me the serenity to accept the things I cannot change,
the courage to change the things I can,
and the wisdom to know the difference. "
~ Serenity Prayer

Without Danny in my life, and cut free from the emotional strings tugging at my heart, I grew stronger. I was able to step back and make unbiased observations of who I was. I gained the courage to uncover deep-rooted untruths, such as believing that Danny's affairs were due to something I had done. This belief was reinforced when he left me for Generosa. I felt abandoned and rejected because I thoroughly believed he did not love me, when in truth it was *me* who didn't love me. Over time I came to the realization that the tears I shed and the overwhelming grief I felt when Danny chose the fork in the road that didn't include me, went much deeper. His leaving me, coldly walking out the door, and divorcing me, as devastating as it was, was the catalyst I needed to release all the emotions I had stuffed over the years.

Trapped feelings gushed forth like a broken dam. I chiseled deep into my psyche and uncovered some qualities about myself that were initially difficult to look at. It was as if I took a large magnifying glass and scrutinized every flaw and blemish of my character. What I saw, although painful, helped me to understand why I allowed myself to remain in an abusive relationship. One of the first things I discovered was that I was addicted to Danny, just as addicted as the smoker who sucks nicotine through a hole in his throat and drags an oxygen tank around for survival. In my addiction, I had accepted the unacceptable. I built walls around my heart and denied what I saw and believed. I blindly ignored Danny's affairs, he had his girlfriends and he had me, other women had become a part of our marriage. Even after Danny married Generosa he continued to behave as if we were still married, I went along with the delusion even though he had another wife. Other people could see him for what he was, but I couldn't. I was completely incapable of acknowledging Danny's lack of morals. Like those crazy mirrors at a carnival, I had a distorted view of him. Divorced or not, I remained emotionally tied to him no matter what he did or where he was.

After months of soul-searching, dissecting, and analyzing I came to realize that I did not do anything wrong. I wasn't the cause of Danny's affairs. I was finally done beating myself up. I was done being overcome by the shame and disgrace of being married to a man convicted of murder. A shame I adopted as my own. I have come to understand that I am not accountable for anyone else's actions. I did nothing to be ashamed of. I was a wife. I was a mother. I went to church. I went to work. I helped children. I accept that I have made choices and decisions throughout my life that were not the wisest. I accept that I cannot change or undo one fraction of a second of what occurred in my life. The past is the past. I could easily have harbored resentments and regretted that I spent my life living in a pitiful fantasy, or I could let it go and move on. I chose to move on. In moving on I learned to accept myself exactly the way I am, and accept that I did the best I could. Through acceptance and letting go of the past, I made room for growth and change. Time is healing and time gave me the opportunity to view my life and witness the courage I didn't know I had. I always thought of myself as helpless and weak, too frightened to rock the boat and stand up for myself. But I did. I rocked the boat when I went to Al-Anon, even though it made Danny angry. I rocked some more when I persevered in my education, even though Danny criticized me. I rocked further when I pursued a profession, even though Danny mocked me. I rocked the boat again and changed the course when I made the decision not to attend Danny's trial as I wanted to do. I knew that if I stepped foot in that courtroom, I would have slipped back into the hole that I had slowly crawled out of. Pity for him would have erased from my mind the damage he caused my children and myself. For me to steer clear of the trial and put my self-preservation first was the actual beginning of taking care of myself. When I looked back on all that I did, rather than what I did not do, I was amazed to discover that I possessed an inner strength all along. Me? Strong? I never would have guessed. But, of course. How else could I have come out on the other side still standing on my own two feet? How else would I have found the courage to expedite major decisions, and to have the faith that as I closed one door a new one was waiting for me?

2005 (SEPTEMBER)

MOVING ON

"When one door closes another door opens;
but we so often look so long and so regretfully upon the closed door,
that we do not see the ones which open for us."
~ Alexander Graham Bell

As I physically felt better and grew emotionally stronger, I was able to step over the threshold of fear and bring about life-altering changes. One of the hardest decisions I made was to leave the center that Carol and I had created years before. Carol and I were more than partners; we were close loving friends for years. We were an incredible team. Where I was shy and reserved and preferred to stay in the background, Carol was outgoing and extroverted. When one of us was down, the other could lift her up. We had been together so long that we could read each other's minds and finish the sentence the other one started. We melded together as a single thinking, feeling unit. We grew from two young enthusiastic women with a vision, to two mature equally enthusiastic wiser women with greater visions. We developed an organization that began with little hand puppets that evolved into a quarter-million-dollar corporation. The dream I had of developing my own preschool program became a reality. Yet it came time for me to move on.

The second major step I took was to sell my home, the house my children grew up in, the house they did not want to leave, but that I could no longer afford to keep. The sale of my home was more than the opportunity to purchase a smaller more economical home; it meant letting go of my life with Danny. A new home was symbolic of the new life my family was about to embark on. Packed within the dozens of cardboard boxes was the rancid accumulation of over twenty years of the life experiences of a nuclear family gone sour, like a container of milk left out on a hot summer day.

My most difficult challenge, more difficult than leaving the center or selling my home, was emotionally divorcing myself from Danny. That took a very long time. Anyone who has quit smoking knows that the strong psychological cravings are much worse than the physical withdrawal. Even from faraway prison Danny still tried to control my life, and on more than one occasion I almost let him. He would call from prison and want to speak with me regarding some situation or another, but I used to make my kids lie and tell him I wasn't home. If I did speak with him, I wound up being angry with myself. It was easier for me to find the courage to stand up to the intimidating detectives than it was for me to assert myself with Danny. It was an ongoing struggle for me to keep my guard up and not yield to my self-destructive patterns. Letting go of Danny was liberating. Closing that chapter of my life allowed new wondrous doors to open. After selling my home and purchasing another I decided to take a year off from work, which turned out to be more like a year and a half. I had some money put aside from the sale of my home that afforded me this luxury. I felt I earned this time off. My entire family had been under tremendous stress for too long. We needed time to adjust to the major changes that were taking place. We needed some structure back in our lives. We needed to share our meals, kick our feet up on the couch and sit back, relax and enjoy. I took advantage of my free time to concentrate on completing my doctorate studies. After years of intense study, mounds of research work and a tumultuous chaotic life filled with a frustratingly endless battle of obstacles and stumbling blocks, out of sheer perseverance, I was justly rewarded for my determined efforts and finally granted the title of Doctor of Education. It was the one area in my life that I paid heed to my mother's advice. I promised her on the day that Danny and I came to her as two foolish teenagers wanting to get married that I would continue with my education. I am grateful that I didn't give up as I often wanted to do and for my family and friends who continually encouraged me to stay with it.

Taking time away from the work world had other added benefits as well - like raising a baby. At forty-three years of age, I found myself raising a baby again. Seline is my half-sister, we share the same father. My father remarried some years after my mother divorced him. I was happy my father had picked up the pieces after his divorce and found someone to share his life with, but due to unforeseen circumstances, my father and his wife were not able to raise their own daughter. Seline was less than four months old when I became her permanent guardian, she is now 15. With my own kids grown and independent I thought I was going to be footloose and fancy-free. Obviously, God had other plans for me. I could not turn my back on this tiny little being with a wisp of light blonde hair and big blue trusting eyes, my half-sister. That is not who I am. I call Seline the miracle baby, not just because she survived a difficult birth, but because she seems to work miracles with everyone who comes in contact with her. This precious bundle of sugar and spice and all things nice turns cloudy days bright. Whenever I found myself overwhelmed or concerned about the future, one baby bear hug from my little sibling and all my problems fade away. I know I have a lifetime of challenges ahead of me, but I have no regrets in my decision.

As for my three children they have each had a portion of their youth snatched from them that can never be replaced, special occasions spoiled by sadness and confusion. The impact of Danny's conviction will have a permanent effect on them for the rest of their lives. Each has had to deal with it and the events that led to it according to their own coping ability and how each was affected by their father's inconsistency throughout their lives. They have come a long way from the day their father walked out, but it's been a very rough road. There were more than a few fathers who would not let their daughters go out with my sons, minor incidents with the law that other kids might have received a slap on the wrist and a strong warning turned into major legal matters for both my sons involving costly lawyers and stiff penalties, all because of who their father is. In Al-Anon I learned that alcoholism is a family disease, to me, this is the same theory. One member may be behind bars, but all family members suffer. My children, all adults now, periodically visit their father in prison for special occasions like Christmas or Father's Day.

The detectives believed that Danny made a drunken confession to me and that I out of fear protected him. Contrary to what the detectives assumed, I do not know what took place on that dreadful night of October 21, 2001, my son Tony's eleventh birthday and I am done obsessing over whether or not Danny committed this vicious crime. I have had to let this lingering mystery go in order to move on with my life.

As an interesting side note, on April 8, 2005, after two years of anguish, and thousands of dollars in attorney fees, the LIPA charge was dismissed; justice was finally obtained. My fingerprints and mug shots have been removed from the police files as if the arrest never existed, but the trauma from this fiendish experience remains. My heart still races whenever I see a police car behind me. It was never determined who was in my basement in April of 2002.

2005- PRESENT

RECIPE TO EMPOWER YOUR LIFE

"There are no mistakes, no coincidences.
All events are blessings given to us to learn from."
~ Elisabeth Kubler-Ross

Not long after completing my doctorate and obtaining guardianship of Seline, I was thrilled to find a position as director of a prominent daycare-preschool center where I could use my newly achieved degree and years of working with children. So instead of taking Seline for long leisurely walks that I had become accustomed to, I was taking her on a two-hour ride on the snail-paced Long Island Expressway to work with me, the major perk to my job. My experience with young children was a tremendous asset to this new challenging position that had over three hundred children in attendance. The women who worked in the surrounding areas began to find their way to my office, first for work-related problems and then for personal matters. They learned to trust me. It was as if I had a revolving door, no sooner did one-person leave than another came asking advice or consolation. And it wasn't just the adults; the children flocked to me as if I was the Pied Piper himself, especially those who had been labeled with behavior problems. I realized I had become the peacemaker, the mediator, the person who actually listened to the complaints and did something about them. When the women eventually discovered that I was the ex-wife of the infamous convicted murderer, that I had once been arrested, and that I, like them, was a single struggling parent, and that I managed to pick myself up from the bottom of the pit, they gathered around me even more. They didn't come to hear about the gossip or the trial, or whether or not I thought Danny was guilty; they came because they wanted to know how I survived, how I could laugh and be positive after what I had experienced. They told me they wanted what I had. I was stunned. I wasn't aware I had come that far. I thought I was still plodding along waiting for the day when things would get better.

Pastor Lydia's words from years before came to mind; *God was going to use my experience in a way I could never imagine.* For years I wondered how someone who was as broken as I was could help anyone else. But on reflection on a rainy drive home, I saw that my experiences were indeed helping others. Daily words of encouragement had evidently benefited this small group of women so much. How had I gone from that sad, confused, helpless victim I saw myself as to a fairly confident self-assured woman? The transformation didn't happen in a week, a month, or even a year. I was ready to step out of my comfort zone and reach out to help other women. Except, it didn't happen exactly the way I thought. In fact, it didn't happen. I had completed the original *Recipe to Empower Your Life*, except for some minor adjustments, but when it came time to publish it, I put it under my bed, where it sat for *thirteen years*. I could say life got in the way, which it did to a certain degree, but in hindsight, I wasn't ready. There were more of life's twists and turns. It is not predictable. The journey is not always an easy one. Life is a complex maze of challenges, questions, doubts, opportunities, setbacks, failures, successes, risks, triumphs, gambles, luck, fortune and faith. I experienced all of these during this span of time, including some major material losses, such as my adorable little house that went into foreclosure, my new car was repossessed, and bills were accumulating to the point I could not handle, due to extensive attorney and court fees. I was always juggling money, borrowing from Peter to pay Paul. This became my way of living. It was exhausting. But I continued to do what I had to do to survive being a single mom, with no child support, with two growing teenage boys and a young child.

Living on one income on Long Island is a disaster in the making. But as devastating as these losses were, they were nothing in comparison to the death of my father, who passed away suddenly in 2010 without having any life insurance, which added to my financial burden. Two months later, on the eve of Thanksgiving, my beautiful niece died at the tender age of nineteen from a tragic car accident. Overload for sure! Compound all of this with a sixty-hour work week and a three-hour commute, (with a baby!), from the eastern end of Long Island to Nassau County for the eight years I was director of the Early Childhood Educational Center. To say I was physically, emotionally, and spiritually exhausted is putting it mildly. When a position as a Site Director for an Alternative High School program was offered to me which was close to my home with the same hours as a school calendar, I jumped at the chance. Although it was not in the early childhood field, I accepted the position. The students who were enrolled were mandated by a judge to attend. This program was their last chance before the judge would remove them from their homes and place them in Juvenile Detention, a group home or even incarceration. I saw the program as a time for the students to press restart. It was intimidating at first, these adolescents were defiant juvenile delinquents with criminal charges, were truant, hated school, hated authority, hated their lives, some were aggressive, and others substance abusers. But I was excited to take on the new challenge. I honestly had no clue how all my early childhood experience would come into play with this position. I quickly learned these adolescents were in fact still children who felt the world gave up on them. They needed someone to listen to them without judgment, they needed to be respected, encouraged, challenged, guided and accepted. This program changed the trajectory for many of them, not all, some didn't make it and moved into group homes or were incarcerated. But it was my job to continue to do what I was doing and hope that for the ones that didn't make it, some seeds were planted that hopefully one day they could use.

I guess it's fair to say I've had a few of these curveballs thrown at me over the years. With each episode, I had a choice. I could either view my situation as a hopeless disaster or I could uncover some hidden part of me and find out who I really was and what I wanted to do with my life. Well, my opportunity, my *gift*, came wrapped in very rough sandpaper. Ouch! Not one to give up or give in, I reached for my strong faith when I was given a pink slip and told that not only was my position as Site Director for the alternative program for at-risk adolescents terminated, but the entire program was canceled. I ran through the whole gamut of emotions in less than a minute. I was angry, furious actually, frustrated, concerned for my financial stability, and deeply saddened because I saw the value of this program, things didn't make sense. I was finally in a stable job, with a retirement plan, health insurance, and benefit days and close to home. How could it be over, just like that? Thirty days later, the doors closed. In rapid succession the old fears took hold. What was I going to do? What did I want to do? Questions flooded my brain like a category 4 hurricane, swirling and twirling the confused thoughts. I knew I was at a turning point in my life, I just didn't know where I was turning. After days of reeling fury and woeful sobbing, the only thing I knew was that I had no control, and I had to trust the process of uncertainty. I did not want to venture down that road again. I applied for several positions, but my experience required a higher salary than an entry-level position. I was either overqualified or underqualified. I honestly didn't know how I was going to find a job, let alone a job that I loved. I quickly went through my meager savings. It was an extremely difficult time. I remember one particular day when I went food shopping and had to put several items back because I didn't have enough money to pay for them. When I got home while unloading the packages, the laundry soap fell out of the back of my car onto the graveled driveway, the top broke off, and the detergent drained into the gravel. I frantically scooped the oozing liquid up with the cap and put it back into the container, gravel and all. I didn't have the money to buy another. I didn't know how hitting this low place was going to be my greatest gift.

Not having to go to a job everyday gave me plenty of luxury of time. I had discovered a wonderful path in the woods that ends up at the bay. It soon became my favorite place. There's something magical about this path, it is my serenity, my sanctuary, it is my church. One early morning the fog hovered low over the trees. It was like heaven touching the earth. The brilliant autumn sun sparkled through the colorful leaves. In that moment I knew I was going to be ok. I was right where I needed to be. The sounds, sights and smells of nature, healed me. In this blissful quietness, I breathed, prayed and heard what I needed to hear. I would often sit on a bench gazing at the bay, reviewing my life and trying to figure out how it all connected. Sometimes the bay was as still as a sheet of glass, soothing my restless mind. Other times the water was rough and choppy with white foaming waves pounding the beach. My emotions were like the tide, rising and falling. Nothing stays the same. At times life is calm and at others it is rough. Many days I sat there for hours, meditating on the perplexity of my life purpose. On one particular day, I looked down and saw a beautifully heart-shaped rock. I firmly believe that our loved ones come to us in special ways when we need them the most, like my brother-in-law and the pennies. Now, my niece, Candice comes to me in magnificently heart-shaped rocks, so it was not a surprise to find this rock on that day. When Candice passed away, I found a heart-shaped rock, a friend of mine cut the rock in half, I put one half in her casket and the other sits on my dresser in my bedroom. Since that day I find heart rocks just when I need them.

This journey hasn't been an easy one; it required persistence, self-discipline, fortitude and faith. When I received the notice that my program was shutting down and I would be unemployed, my mother said to me, "congratulations now you can do what you were meant to do." I was puzzled. What am I meant to do? "Finish writing your book," Mom answered. I questioned whether I was ready to complete and publish the book. I wanted to wait until I was all better, until I had all the answers and didn't make any more mistakes. I wasn't quite ready to do that, so I chose a safer subject to write about, one that I was an expert at. I developed a book for teachers on how to manage challenging behaviors in a classroom, "Recipe for Creating a Peaceful Classroom," which included a 14-hour educational course to go along with the book. I also created my own coaching and consulting business, "Polaris Coaching and Consulting Services." As I taught teachers and interacted with other women, I could see how I still had the ability to touch and inspire them, just as I had while working at the Early Childhood Center.

My dear friend Annie asked me to give a talk at her *Finding Your Own Passion Workshop* about how I went about writing my memoir. I accepted her offer, not knowing what I was really going to talk about, but I brought my two self-published books. When I started to tell my life story and all that I had overcome, it became instantly clear that life isn't about never making mistakes, it's about evolving, coping, accepting, forgiving, healing, gratitude and paying it forward. It's about lemons and ingredients and being the best chef you can be. It is the recipe to empower your life. My story can be someone else's survival guide. My experience can help another person. My life and all the ups and downs, all the chaos, all the loss, is truly a gift. I am happier than I have ever been. More grateful, more joyful, more peaceful, more confident and no longer ashamed. I have awoken and am finally aligned with my life's purpose. The answers were always in me, I just needed to believe in myself.

I hope my story will help you see that no matter your circumstances, no matter your age, your education, how many times you've been knocked down, or how many times you tried to make a change, but couldn't, it actually is possible. What matters is how many times you get back up. I know because I've done it. I hope these words do more than inspire you; I hope they motivate you to make changes in yourself because your life *will* change. You're not going to finish the book and be cured. But it's a starting point. One sentence at a time, One page at a time. And that is how it will go. So, are you ready? Only you can make that decision.

Just as my dear friend Joy had said years earlier that life was handing me some big fat lemons, so if I was going to survive, I had better whip up a big batch of lemonade. Joy had said it as a joke that New Year's weekend in the Bahamas, but when I thought about the old adage, the wheels that are forever spinning in my brain spun some more, and the visual of a recipe began to emerge. If I could turn lemons into lemonade, why not turn those sour situations, (feelings, emotions, attitudes, behaviors) into something better than lemonade, why not something sweeter, like a savory lemon meringue pie. That was something I could relate to. If negative feelings and behaviors were what I referred to as *lemons*, (anger, blame, resentment, negative beliefs, fear, shame, depression, anxiety, procrastination, perfection, guilt, people-pleasing), then they needed to be replaced with some delectable *ingredients*, also known as positive feelings and behaviors, (courage, gratitude, faith, self-love, self-awareness, acceptance, forgiveness, boundaries, responsibility, positive thinking, communication, humor, family and friends, life purpose), that could nourish, nurture, replenish and empower every area of life. Positive emotions work collectively, like the ingredients in a recipe. A wise chef understands the relation of spices, how each spice enhances the taste of the other and if even one is omitted, there is a lack to the taste buds. This book uses the same approach, each of the positive enriching *ingredients* need to be a part of the batter in that huge mixing bowl of life in order to manifest your dreams and fulfill your life purpose. You can't change the past, but by exploring, identifying and understanding what the *lemons* are in your life today, you can create an incredible tomorrow. Thus, *Recipe to Empower Your Life* was created to teach *you* how to be the *chef* of your own life. Through my own self-discovery and my own healing, I found a way to guide other women who are much like me. The events of my past, as Pastor Lydia said, would not be in vain. I can help others because I've been there.

PART II

RECIPE TO EMPOWER YOUR LIFE

"There is only one corner of the universe you can be certain of improving and that is your own self."
~ Aldous Huxley

For those of you on a journey to finding empowerment, self-love and acceptance the words on these pages are dedicated to you, to help you see the beauty that is staring back at you in the mirror, to find the strength to conquer your heartbreak, to gain the confidence to eliminate your insecurities and to remind you that YOU are an incredible warrior of strength.

The gateway to change is first to become aware and understand what *lemons* hold you back from being the extraordinary person you were meant to be. Holding onto my *lemons,* kept me small. It was what I thought I deserved. They validated that I was not good enough. *Lemons* are like weeds in a garden. Before flowers or vegetables can be planted, the weeds need to be removed; otherwise, they will overtake the garden. *Lemons,* unlike weeds, are not necessarily removed, they are brought to the surface of awareness. Awareness opened the door in acknowledging, accepting and releasing my *lemons*; the *lemons* of *shame, fear, anger, resentment, blame, negative beliefs, perfectionism, guilt, people-pleasing, anxiety, depression and procrastination.* That's quite the list. But what was I supposed to do with this newfound knowledge? Being aware was a good place to start, but it wasn't going to change anything. How was I going to move from shame and fear and all the other lemons? As my mind slowly began to absorb what I was learning, I thought of the weeds in a garden. For flowers to flourish they need space to grow. By clearing out my *lemons*, I was then able to add the key ingredients of *faith, courage, gratitude, self-love, positive thinking, self-responsibility, communication, humor* and a *loving support network.*

The thought of changing life-long beliefs and behaviors was frightening and overwhelming. It was a process, and it continues to be a process. Martin Luther King said, "if you can't fly, then run, if you can't run, then walk, if you can't walk, then crawl, but whatever you do you have to keep moving forward." You don't have to see the whole staircase to take the first step. One simple step at a time, it is a give and take, a release and an add. I am the chef of my life, how liberating and empowering is that! But it required showing up for life and doing the unpleasant work. And believe me, digging through the muck was unpleasant, and often painful.

The key to empowerment is not necessarily how we obtained our *lemons*, but in determining what they are. The *lemons* in our life are there for a reason. Even the very negative ones serve a purpose and offer a measure of comfort. It is a feeling that is familiar to us. It is much easier to blame others for our predicament or to believe that we are the victim and are powerless. But holding onto such negative behaviors keeps us bound within that small box we have created in order to feel safe.

In time we are able to understand that the *lemons* of negative emotions that we have come to identify ourselves with, don't mean that we are these feelings, they are only feelings and we are merely the observer of these feelings. Today I own my story, but I no longer have to be defined by it. In the end, it's not what I have been through that defines who I am, it is how I got through it, how I sculpted the person I am today and the person I am capable of being tomorrow. Instead of looking at myself as shattered, I am a mosaic of the battles I have won. The light shines through the cracks. To move forward I had to add the appropriate *ingredients* that led me to a life of empowerment, which today has brought me freedom, peace and joy. It will take courage and a mighty leap of faith to step out of that box and when you do that will be your first step towards transformation and a life of empowerment.

At the end of each section are exercises that will offer you healing and personal growth. Each section speaks about my personal experiences with my own *lemons* and how I have applied the positive *ingredients* to my life. Through these exercises you will discover your lemons or negative behaviors, each exercise will help you delve a little deeper and begin the process of peeling your lemons. The questions have been designed to help you understand why you behave the way you do. The ingredient questions will help you recognize your positive qualities, what your strengths are and which ingredient needs another teaspoon or two. Each ingredient has the potential to bring you closer to a life of joy and empowerment.

Following are a list of the healing practices that I've used. Each offers its own unique healing therapy, most can be done on your own with a little effort on your part, a few require a professional of the field. I suggest, over time, you try them all and discover for yourself which ones you feel the most benefit from.

HEALING PRACTICES

Journaling - is simply writing down your thoughts and feelings. I found this simple, uncomplicated exercise had the potential of unleashing pent-up emotions. Sometimes I would be writing furiously, angry over something, only to discover the anger was caused by deep sadness and old unresolved hurt. Or just the opposite, I would be writing about the sadness I felt, which turned out stemmed from anger. I highly recommend journaling, it is a way to help you tap into what is going on beneath the surface, and to see the progress you are making.

Gratitude List - to keep you focused upon thankfulness. One of the best ways to lift my spirit and bring myself out of depression or fear/worry, was to write down what I was grateful for. In the beginning, I listed every single thing I was grateful for, the ability to see, to hear, to smell, my legs, my hands, a running car, fuel in the tank, food in the refrigerator, I covered pages and pages and was amazed of how much I had to be thankful for. I found this practice helpful to use before I went to bed to help me sleep better. I would list five things that I was grateful for, five things different from the night before, the sunset one night, the rain nourishing the earth, another night. At my lowest moments, it was extremely difficult to list even one thing. But I persisted and it never failed, by the time I was ready to turn off the light, I often had more than five. This had become a daily practice to help my mind shift to an attitude of gratitude. I still use this today, I may not write it down on paper, but in my mind, especially when I'm sitting quietly by the water, I go over my many gifts. You can be really creative and decorate a notebook with happy pictures or drawings, use colored pens and pencils and happy stickers.

· · ·

EFT - Emotional Freedom Technique – also referred to as tapping on the meridians of the body, the same meridians an acupuncturist uses or also psychological acupressure. This technique is believed to create a balance in the energy system.

I had used **EFT** several times. At the beginning, I needed a practitioner to show me where and how to tap and guide me with words that would help bring my feelings to the surface. The practitioner was one of the kindest and soft-spoken women I've ever known. The theory of tapping along the meridians helps to release whatever the negative belief might be and replace it with positive feelings/emotions. At the end of the session, I would feel a great sense of balance and peace. I would feel lighter as if a heavy backpack of emotions were lifted. After a while, I learned to do this on my own and have also taught Seline how to use this powerful healing technique. I highly recommend it.

Transformational Breath - an active exercise that uses the breath to release tension within the body. It opens up the respiratory system. When the breath is restricted, there can be physical, mental and emotional ailments.

One of the therapies/exercises I used to help me with my deep feelings of shame, fear and anger, was Transformational Breath. Years of tension that was stored in my body slowly began to be released in these very powerful and intense sessions. On my first session, the practitioner said my breathing was so restricted and shallow, she said it was as if I didn't feel I deserved to be alive or take up space on earth. That was true. That was how much I disliked myself. During the session as life events passed through my mind, my body would become rigid and my breathing restricted. The practitioner, in her kind and gentle voice, helped me purge and release these overwhelming emotions. It would have taken years of counseling to get the results I got in a one-hour session. I continued with several sessions until I felt a substantial release and my breathing became more balanced.

Reiki - is a Japanese method for relaxation that relies on the concept that a "life force energy" flows inside of us. Reiki is a form of healing; a practitioner places their hands on or near a person's body to eliminate negative energy.

Reiki is another amazing healing therapy. I attended many Reiki circles. In some circles there were many people and several Reiki practitioners that would rotate from person to person, and in some circles there were just a few. It didn't matter how many people were there, the end result was always the same. When the practitioner would place their hands over my body, I would feel a tremendous energy surging through me. Sometimes I would feel very hot. By the end of the session, I always felt extremely peaceful and relaxed.

Positive Affirmations & Visualization - are the practices of positive thinking and self-empowerment using positive phrases or statements to challenge negative or unhelpful thoughts. Visualization is a technique for creating images in your mind to manifest your wants, goals and desires.

I've used vision boards to help me stay focused on my goals. It was fun creating the poster. I'd cut out words from magazines, like LOVE, or EATING HEALTHY, and pictures of a healthy balanced meal, or an ad from a spa about massage, or a yoga posture. I'd draw dollar signs all over the poster and the words like MONEY, WEALTH, or FINANCIAL INDEPENDENCE. Whatever I wanted and hoped for, I'd put on the poster.

I'd tape positive affirmations on my bathroom or bedroom mirror, or taped them to my car console, refrigerator, even over my kitchen sink, inspiring quotes—*"If you can dream it, you can have it," "All Glory comes from Daring to Begin",* and of course the *Serenity Prayer,* and so many more. I'm a collector of inspirational quotes!

Mindfulness - is a mental state achieved by focusing one's awareness on the present moment, while calmly acknowledging and accepting one's feelings, thoughts, and bodily sensations.

When I found myself worrying about the future or fretting over the past, I would recognize that I wasn't living in the present moment. I'd take a deep breath and do my best to be fully aware of the very moment I was in, even if that moment was uncomfortable. At the times I was actually able to achieve that level of being in the moment, (it's an ongoing process!) I could literally feel my body relax. When we think about a dog, as an example, they live truly and completely in the moment, no worries about their health, money, relationships, nothing but the moment they are in. I love the quote, "keep your head where your feet are."

Meditation - is a practice where an individual uses a technique such as mindfulness or focusing the mind on a particular object, thought, or activity, to train attention and awareness and achieve a mentally clear and emotionally calm and stable state.

Meditation and mindfulness go pretty much hand in hand. You need mindfulness to meditate and meditation to be mindful. Or basically, to be aware, aware of the moment, aware of feelings, aware of thoughts. You don't necessarily need to sit in a lotus position with incense burning to meditate, all you need to do is quiet the mind and be aware of the moment.

Service - doing helpful acts to serve someone else, with no expectations. Pay it forward–passing on the kindness received to oneself by being kind to someone else.

Years ago, when I was in desperate need of a car, my brother offered me one that he had. He could easily have sold it, but he chose to GIVE it to me, a gesture I found humbling. Finally, years later, the day came when I was able to purchase my own, new car. I had been driving a Honda with over 220,000 miles. I, like my brother, could have sold it for a few dollars, but I found out about a woman, a single woman doing her best to take care of her family, and offered her the Honda. That car with all those miles changed the woman's life, gave her some independence, just like the car from my brother changed my life. It is a great joy to do service for another. It is one of the most rewarding things we can do.

Connection- connecting with nature, family & friends.

I believe one of my most healing therapies is the deep connection I have with nature. Those daily walks down my favorite path opened my eyes and my heart to all the beauty around me. Sometimes the water would be so overwhelmingly beautiful, I'd cry. Or a turtle would meander across the path, or I'd spot a deer watching me from the distance. Whatever it was, filled me with such great joy and peacefulness.

One of my greatest gifts is the close and loving relationship I have with each of my children, and my mom. And now I have four amazing, funny, delightful grandchildren who live close by. I love our times together and our sleepovers. As exhausting as they are, I wouldn't trade these special times. Not everyone is blessed to have loving positive relationships with their biological family, often our friends are our family, and that is okay. As long as we stay connected.

I continue to use these healing therapies, some more than others, when I feel out of balance, or a strong emotion has surfaced and I need to find out what triggered it. Of course, the one I use the most is **Connection,** predominantly my walks in nature on my favorite path. It is so much a part of my life now that I don't think I could ever not connect to nature or family and friends.

I hope this book will be able to lead you on the path to a happy full life. You deserve it. Are you ready to become the chef of your own life?

NOTES

LEMONS & INGREDIENTS

Release Lemons of:
Fear, Shame, Anger, Blame, Resentment

Add Ingredients of:
Courage, Faith, Forgiveness, Acceptance, Hope

Healing Practice:
Connection, Transformational Breath

"If we do not change our direction,
we are likely to end up where we are headed."
~ Ancient Chinese Proverb

I scrutinized my *lemons* of *fear, shame, blame* and *resentment* and how they manifested in my daily life, with such intense fervor, as if I were a forensic investigator. There are so many types of *fear;* fear of confrontations, fear of abandonment, fear of failure, fear of success, fear of commitment, fear of rejection, fear of what others may think, fear of making a mistake, fear of lack of control. Fear ruled my life. I was living through a fear-based lens. Every choice, decision, response, reaction, word, or thought, was fear-based. My life was paralyzed by fear. I was terrified to be alone and to be a single mother. I was so fearful of being financially dependent that I resorted to the humiliating behavior of pleading on my hands and knees for my husband not to leave. *Fear* rapidly escalated to living in a constant state of anxiety. Anxious about an uncertain future, anxious about everything that could possibly go wrong. I thought if I worried enough maybe the outcome would be better. Of course, worrying didn't change anything. It merely zapped me of my strength. Chronic anxiety eventually led to poor health, sleepless, fitful nights and sheer exhaustion. I knew I could not go on this way. I was of no use to myself or my children who desperately needed me. I needed to muster up the *courage* to take out my magnifying glass and delve into my inner self. As I started to unpeel my *lemons,* I discovered *I* played a part in my own life, *I* kept myself in the victim mentality. I learned a long time ago that *fear* meant *False Evidence Appearing Real.* I learned the highest form of *courage* is the ability to face our fears, recognize what it is we are fearful of and still proceed. As Mark Twain said, "courage is not the absence of fear; it is acting in spite of it." *Courage* is the quality

148

of state of mind or spirit enabling one to face danger or hardship with confidence and resolution. *Courage* is the ability to face what we think is difficult or painful.

C - Change

O - Openness

U - Understanding

R - Responsibility

A - Awareness/Acceptance/Action

G - Gratitude

E - Empowerment.

It definitely took *courage* for me to feel the *fear* and continue to proceed. It took *courage* to explore the darkness, for then I discovered the power of my light. It took *courage* to give myself permission to start to heal, to make mistakes, to not be perfect, to forgive myself, to reach out for help, to step out of my comfort zone. I stepped out of my comfort zone, big time, when I took the job in New Hyde Park, a two-hour drive on the dreadful Long Island Expressway. It took *courage* for me to drive a hundred miles a day, all the way into Nassau County, me who was always terrified to drive out of my little town. It took tremendous courage when driving home from work on one dark and very snowy blizzard-like evening, with 3-year-old Seline in the backseat watching a video, when suddenly the motor for the windshield wipers stopped working, leaving me without any wipers at all. In most cases, you could pull your car over and wait for help, but highway officials wanted the roads clear for emergencies. I crept along at a snail's pace, gripped to the steering wheel, straining to see out the window.

I used one of Seline's diapers to wipe the windshield, literally hanging out the window. Passing trucks blast me with heavy wet snow. It was extremely dangerous. I called my mother to tell her my dilemma, not sure what she could do hours away. She pleaded with me to pull over and she would come and get me, but I told her that wasn't possible. I was determined to make it home, even in the middle of a snowstorm without a windshield wiper. Thank god the defrosters and heater were working, but it was freezing. I managed to keep a tiny portion of the windshield clear enough for me to see where I was going. My mother kept calling me (thank god for cell phones), checking on me. I had been on the road for five hours, with a tired, cold and hungry little girl. Some may call what I did insane, some may say I was courageous, either would probably be right. But I was determined to get home. I persevered, driving a small distance at a time, wiping the windshield and plowing on. Terrified, but determined. It took *courage* for me to change my familiar behaviors. It took *courage* to speak to homicide detectives, it took *courage* to speak with school officials and defend my children, it took *courage* to break my silence, it took *courage* to stand up for what I believed in. My greatest challenges were my greatest gifts to learn from and it is *courage* that helped me achieve them. It took *courage* to take the mighty leap of faith.

Fear isn't a lack of *courage* as it is a lack of *faith*. For me, *faith* was a belief in the unseen knowing that something positive would happen even if there was no tangible evidence to support this. *Faith* is a belief in something greater than who we are. We may call it God, the Higher Power, the Inner Self, Great Spirit, Divine Intelligence, or any name or title that helps when our spirit is ebbing. Think of *faith* as a bird sitting on a tree branch. The bird is not afraid the branch will break because, for the bird, trust is not in the branch, but in its own wings. It was deep *faith* that Carol and I would accomplish our dreams. It was *faith* that we would sell enough merchandise to purchase the puppets we needed. *Faith* helped lift the weight from my shoulders, helped me navigate the storms, made the impossible possible, it gave me *hope*. And *hope* for me was being able to see that there was light despite the darkness. *Faith* brought me a sense of inner peace, even in the chaos of life. *Faith* calmed my endless mind chatter. Sometimes I had to borrow *faith* from others, and that was okay. The truth was I had everything I needed for the day, maybe not what I wanted, but I did have what I needed. I could not put one toe over the line into the future or the next day. When I felt *fear*, I knew I had to reach out to my support system and connect with my God in order to renew my *faith* and *hope*. I could accept all was good for the day, put my intentions out into the universe, and pray for guidance and support. Maya Angelou, an incredibly wise and spiritual woman, said, "hope and fear cannot occupy the same space at the same time. Invite one to stay." I had a choice, I could live in a paralyzed state of *fear*, insecurity and lack of fulfillment or I could invite trust, *hope* and *faith* to transform my life. I chose hope/faith as my source of power to deal with the unknown in my life. It is not easy. It is a daily practice. I am grateful that I only visit *fear* for a little while, I am not camping out there any longer. When I stay in the place of faith, trust and hope, I can breathe. I can enjoy the simple things in life. I am empowered to keep moving forward.

I often refer back to one of the many slogans in my early days of Al-Anon, "Let Go and Let God." I had to let go of so many things. In some cases, literally, like my house and the center Carol and I founded. I had to let go of trying to control the outcome of an event. I wasn't sure how I was going to complete my doctorate, where the money was coming from to pay my bills, how I was going to raise another baby. What I do know is that when I stopped running, and connected to my higher power, my answers came in the most extraordinary ways, sometimes overhearing strangers' conversations, or a song on the radio, or that one sentence in a book that grabs your attention, or a penny in an unusual place, or a perfect heart-shaped rock. When I begin to feel fearful and doubts creep in, I know my *faith* is down and needs refueling. There are a number of things that I can do to replenish my soul. I can take a walk down my favorite path to connect with God, I can reach out to a friend, I can meditate, sit quietly and focus on my breaths in and out, in and out. I can read a few spiritual passages, and I can review my gratitude list to shift my attitude. Whatever I am dealing with I know I do not have to do it alone. As my spiritual life evolved and I gained trust, amazing things began to happen.

I don't believe there is any other emotion quite as destructive as *shame*. Unfortunately, it had become an all too familiar feeling for me. My *shame* was intense. It's an ugly dirty feeling. A dark secret. It's the I-want-to-crawl-in-a-hole-and-never-come-out-feeling. *Shame* is the reason I couldn't publish this book thirteen years ago. I was drowning in *shame*. I made my ex-husband's behavior and his choices my own. I knew that people judged me for my ex's actions. I had a long history of *shame;* repeatedly accepting my husband back after multiple affairs, the way I begged on my hands and knees for him to stay, three years of living on the sidelines of a sensational publicized murder investigation, and the ultimate murder conviction.

As mortifying as these experiences were nothing compared to the disgrace of being arrested. To be pulled over by a police officer, made to stand outside my car with passing vehicles to witness, have my hands yanked behind my back and handcuffs slapped on, forced into the police car, taken to the police station, fingerprinted, stand for a mug shot and interrogated like a criminal was more degrading than I can even express.

Shame when my face, my mugshot, appeared in the local paper saying I was a thief. These memories are still very vivid in my mind. When I went to work the next day, I didn't speak with anyone, went straight to my office, locked behind a closed door, too ashamed to come out. No one would have guessed how overcome I was with this dark negative feeling that I hid beneath a superficial smile and a neatly tailored suit. It didn't matter how many times I was honored for my good character, dedication and services to the community, *shame* overpowered everything else and took control over my life. It held me back and held me down. As I started to share my deep secrets with trusted people who did not judge me, the secrets lost their power and the *shame* wasn't as overwhelming. Instead of being ashamed of what I went through, today, I am proud of what I have overcome. When *shame* does occasionally rear its ugly head in one form or another, I can work my way through it. It's a daily practice.

Anger. Sometimes *anger* is a necessary emotion. *Anger* can bring action. Get you moving. But seething *anger* is another story. And I was seething. Boiling. Fuming. The *anger* I felt toward my ex-husband for what he put my children and myself through, was dangerous. I was so angry that I couldn't change the circumstances, that my life was spiraling out of control. I hated him. I hated myself for being an idiot. Sometimes *anger* can be healthy, but nothing good can ever come from hate. Hate keeps you bound emotionally. "Let no man pull you so low as to hate him," Martin Luther King, said. I let that heavy burdensome hate pull me down. That hate brought me a sick satisfaction that my ex-husband was going to spend the rest of his life behind bars, that he lost the honor of walking his only daughter down the aisle, that he would never witness the priceless moments of his grandchildren, that he wouldn't be there to see his sons grow to manhood. I wanted him to suffer as we suffered. Because I wasn't able to address my *anger*, I blamed him for everything. Not that he was innocent because he wasn't, but I had to look at my part and hold myself accountable for my actions and inactions. *Blame* was a waste of time, no matter how much fault I found in Danny and regardless of how much I blamed him, it didn't help me, it didn't change me, it didn't make my life better.

Whenever we point the finger of *blame*, three fingers point back at us. These three fingers can serve as a reminder that we are responsible for our own choices and decisions. With *blame*, I gave up my power. Being accountable, gave me power. Blaming was a way for me to release the pain, but not take responsibility. The more I blamed, the more resentful I became. I expended a lot of energy focusing on what I had to be resentful for, wasting precious moments holding on to past hurts. *Resentment* kept me a prisoner of the past, turned me into a bitter, powerless victim. It stole my self-respect and dignity and kept me at a spiritual standstill. There are no justified resentments, holding onto resentments hurt me the most. As the expression goes, "Anger rots the container that holds it." Anger, blame, and resentment robbed me of my energy, depleted my immune system leading to physical ailments such as ulcers, weight loss and headaches. The more I held on the sicker I got physically, mentally, emotionally and spiritually. I reached my bottom.

Something had to change and that something was me. I had a choice; I could stay stuck in the misery or I could face reality and begin to dissolve the residue that had accumulated over the years. I know I needed to accept and forgive, primarily myself. *Acceptance* didn't mean I surrendered, it didn't mean I was waving the white flag and giving up, it didn't mean I accepted the abuse or mistreatment or that I condoned the behavior, it meant coming to terms with what I could and could not change. I recited the powerful Serenity Prayer daily, sometimes hourly, *"God grant me the serenity to accept the things I cannot change, the courage to change the things I can and the wisdom to know the difference."* I accepted I could not change one second of the past. I couldn't change decisions that I made and wished I hadn't made. I could not go back and undo anything. It happened; it was over. I could not change what I said or what I did or how I acted. The past is the past, even if the past is only ten minutes before. Nothing I could do would change anything. But to accept myself and the experiences and learn from them, that I could do. I had to accept myself, exactly the way I was, my flaws, my imperfections, my physical body, my emotions, my desires, my needs, my wants, my opinions, all of me. This is who I am. Self-love is built on *acceptance.* I also had to accept others. I could not change them any more than I could change the past.

Acceptance is changing what I can and the only thing I can change is myself. I have the power to change my thoughts, my feelings, my attitude, my words and how I respond to life's situations. *Acceptance* makes change possible. *Acceptance* can get us through the day. *Acceptance* gives me a sense of serenity. *Acceptance* is empowering. Along with acceptance came the big "F" word. *Forgiveness.* Pastor Lydia said I needed to forgive my ex-husband before I could set myself free, but it was so hard to forgive him. I wanted him to feel just one ounce of the pain I felt. I thought if I stayed angry, this would somehow hurt him. But holding onto *anger* is like drinking poison and waiting for the other person to die. Holding onto this toxic energy was only hurting me. He could care less, and I was falling apart emotionally, physically, and spiritually.

My major undertaking was to forgive myself. Forgive myself for doing the same things over and over again and expecting different results, the definition of insanity. Forgive myself for letting myself be the doormat, forgive myself for believing I was not good enough. Forgive myself for not having boundaries. Forgive myself for..... The list was endless. And my task seemed unsurmountable. *Forgiveness,* like all the other lemons, is not a one-time fix. Like everything else I had learned, it is a step-by-step, hourly process of healing and taking back my power. One of the best tools was journaling. I filled notebooks. Often the handwriting was illegible, scribbling furiously my deepest emotions, words screaming with vulgarities. It was mentally exhausting but liberating.

After so many emotions erupting I needed to be outside. Regardless of the weather. I walked, sometimes for miles with no destination. The air was purifying. I'd walk to the water, sit on my favorite bench, close my eyes, breathe. Still my mind. In the quiet answers came. *Forgiveness* is a change in attitude and state of mind. It is a spiritual practice. It wasn't a sign of weakness, but an act of strength. *Forgiveness* isn't for the other person. It was for me. It did not change the situation, but it changed me. I did not give in, nor did I forget, but I could remember without being bitter, angry and resentful. It freed me to heal all of me, my body, my mind and my spirit. *Forgiveness* opened a pathway to a new place of peace. *Forgiveness* is a necessary step in the healing process. In trying to figure out how I was going to accomplish that daunting task of forgiving Danny, I realized I needed to first forgive myself. That was a major undertaking, I was angrier at myself and hated myself much more than I hated Danny. Forgiving him came easier than loving me. Very gradually over a very long period of time, I grew to like myself, and ever so slowly I learned to love myself and finally *forgiveness* followed. When I was able to let go of those powerful negative emotions of *anger* and *resentment,* my heart opened, and I could forgive myself, then I could forgive Danny.

FEAR EXERCISE:

What are your fears?

_____

_____

What are you afraid to do?

_____

_____

How is fear getting in the way of where you want to go with your life?

_____

_____

Are you able to make necessary decisions when you are fearful?

_____

_____

What do you do when you are filled with fear?

_____

_____

What situations create a feeling of fear for you?

_____

_____

Who are you frightened of?

_____

_____

Is there anyone you feel safe enough to talk to about your fears?

_____

_____

SHAME EXERCISE:

Do you feel shame by an act you did?

_____

_____

Do you feel shame by the act of another person? If so, how do you act towards that individual?

_____

_____

Do your feelings of shame hold you back from seeking help?

_____

_____

Are you carrying feelings of shame from your childhood?

_____

_____

How has the feeling of shame altered your life?

_____

_____

ANGER EXERCISE:

What causes you to become angry? Fear? Resentment? Blame?

_____

_____

Did you express your anger as a child? How?

_____

_____

Were you allowed to express your anger when you were a child?

_____

_____

How did your parents express their anger?

_____

_____

How do you feel when someone is angry with you?

_____

_____

What do you do with those feelings?

_____

_____

Do certain people trigger your anger?

_____

_____

Do you express your anger today? How?

_____

_____

How do you feel after you have expressed your anger? Satisfied? Guilty? Ashamed?

_____

_____

Once you have expressed your anger, are you able to let it go?

_____

_____

What are you learning about your anger?

_____

_____

What would you like to do differently with your anger?

_____

_____

What are some positive ways for you to release your anger?

_____

_____

Healthy expression of anger can result in increased self-esteem.

BLAME EXERCISE:

Are you blaming anyone or any situation for the way your life is today?

_____

_____

Are you blaming anyone for the way your life was in the past?

_____

_____

If so, what are the benefits you receive from placing blame?

_____

_____

RESENTMENT EXERCISE:

Do you resent anyone from the past? Who? Why?

_____

_____

Are you still holding on to those feelings of resentment?

_____

_____

Are these individuals aware that you resent them?

_____

_____

Do you resent anyone today? Who? Why?

_____

_____

Write out the resentments; just keep writing, when you are done writing come back to it and look at what you have written. Who is being hurt? Who needs to be forgiven?

_____

_____

COURAGE EXERCISE:

What does courage mean to you?

_____

_____

Do you feel you are weak?

_____

_____

List the times in your life that you had courage. How did you find that courage?

_____

_____

If you do not feel that you have courage, what do you believe is holding you back?

_____

_____

What behaviors do you want to change that will require courage?

_____

_____

Are you ready to step out of your comfort zone?

_____

_____

ACCEPTANCE EXERCISE:

How do you know when someone's behavior is unacceptable?

_____

_____

How do you let the individual know that their behavior is unacceptable?

_____

_____

Do you feel you accept yourself for who you are? Do you accept your body? Thoughts? Feelings?

_____

_____

Do you accept others for who they are?

_____

_____

Do you feel you have or still are accepting unacceptable behavior?

_____

_____

Are you able to accept that you cannot change the past?

_____

_____

How can you apply the Serenity Prayer in your life? (God grant me the serenity to accept what I cannot change, the courage to change what I can and the wisdom to know the difference.)

_____

_____

What do you have the power to change in your life?

_____

_____

What are the steps you will take?

_____

_____

FORGIVENESS EXERCISE:

Do you feel there are people in your life that have hurt you?

_____

_____

Have you let the person or persons know that their actions have hurt you?

_____

_____

Are you hanging on to bitterness or anger towards another?

_____

_____

What have you done with the feelings of hurt? Do you feel anger? Sadness? Ignore your feelings and pretend they don't exist?

_____

_____

Are you able to forgive these individuals in order to move forward?

_____

_____

Have you hurt anyone by your thoughts, words or actions?

_____

_____

Do you feel you need to forgive yourself? If so, for what?

_____

_____

How will you begin your process of forgiveness?

_____

_____

FAITH EXERCISE:

Do you consider yourself spiritual?

_____

_____

Would you like to develop your spirituality?

_____

_____

In what ways do you bring spirituality into your daily living?

_____

_____

What aspects of your spiritual life do you want to strengthen?

_____

_____

NOTES:

Release Lemons of:

Victim, Perfection/People-Pleasing, Depression, Guilt

Add Ingredients of:

Self-Awareness/Self-Love/Self-Respect/Self-Esteem,
Communication, Accountability, Boundaries, Gratitude

Healing Practice:

Meditation, Journaling

"In the hour of adversity be not without hope, for crystal rain falls from black clouds."

~ Persian Poem

I was feeling disconnected from everything in my life. *Depression* caused this overpowering feeling of hopelessness and unworthiness. I even had suicidal thoughts. I had so many reasons to feel depressed, my shameful publicized divorce, financial stress, my life just not going as I planned. Carrying a heavy load of debilitating feelings of shame, guilt, and fear, along with repressed anger for a number of years, and combining them with a humiliating public divorce, incredible loss, a move, and a husband convicted of murder, went beyond sadness, beyond grief, straight to depression. I felt no joy or peace, it was just one thing after another. I've often heard people say, *God doesn't give you more than you can handle,* but I think I had enough.

I built huge walls around myself to keep sadness and heartbreak out, but in reality, it also kept the joy out. Even with a strong clinical background I never recognized that I was deeply despondent. I was living under the myth that as long as I showered, dressed, applied my make-up and went to work, then I must be fine. What I didn't notice was the effort it took to get out of bed in the morning. Or that it took more make-up to cover the dark circles under my eyes. But I had no choice. I had to get up. I had to go to work. I had a family to support and bills to pay. I avoided friends and any sort of socialization. I isolated myself from just about everyone. I had no appetite and dropped a significant amount of weight. I couldn't put food in my mouth without gagging. I was physically run down and emotionally numb. It wasn't possible to care for my physical body when emotionally I saw no light at the end of the tunnel, just one constant hovering dark cloud. I had long before passed the stage of uncontrollable crying. My life consisted of work and home. What saved me from going over the deep end was concentrating on a doctorate program that I entered in the middle of the most stressful time of my life. Everyone thought I was nuts. Maybe I was. But focusing on my studies kept me from succumbing to the overwhelming pain and sadness that I believed would never go away. Time helped of course. Nothing is forever. Time and putting my energy into writing endless reports for my doctorate program were primary factors in helping me keep a grip on myself. Little by little feelings of hopefulness sprouted through the bleakness. I began to feel better, eat better and get a decent night's sleep. I wasn't waking every night from a horrible nightmare. I lived by the motto, "one day at a time" and one day at a time I healed, grew stronger, physically, mentally and emotionally. Although I knew that *depression* is unresolved anger, anger turned inward, I wasn't able to identify it in me.

The circumstances in my life provided me with the excuse I needed to feel sorry for myself. Every aspect of my life was falling apart. I felt stuck and unable to help myself until I heard it is when things look the darkest, that I had the power to change what I was feeling by finding *gratitude*. Most days I was too filled with despair to find anything to be grateful about. The best I could do was recite the Serenity Prayer over and over again. I tried hard to focus on these powerful words, but my mind would be on something negative or some fear would envelop me. There were days I had to force myself to think of something, anything that could create a switch that could turn my thinking around. The more I recognized what I had to be grateful for, the more I was appreciative and thankful for everything, the good, the bad and everything in between. I have learned to turn a negative into a positive.

Gratitude, to me, is the purest emotion. Practicing *gratitude* was a way for me to master shifting my emotions. Once I was able to shift my emotions to an attitude of gratitude, it shifted my entire perception of life. I felt safe enough to stop fighting the current and flow with the tide. Developing an attitude of *gratitude* is one of the best gifts I gave myself. When I opened my heart to this experience, it allowed the energy to flow. Today, because I cultivated an attitude of *gratitude* all my senses are heightened. It is as if I had awoken. For the first time while on my daily walk to the beach I heard the geese wings flapping as they flew overhead. I smelled wood burning in fireplaces as I jogged down the block. I am in awe at the magnificence of the sun setting, and the water gently lapping on the shore. On challenging days, my soul is renewed when walking on my special path. Attitude is everything. It determines our lives. "Attitude is a little thing that makes a big difference," said Winston Churchill.

We are not responsible for the circumstances or events that happen to us, but we are responsible for how we respond to those circumstances and events. It is all in our attitude. An Attitude of Gratitude. I am grateful for every frightening and shameful experience because they made me a stronger, wiser person. Because I lived in darkness for so long, I followed the light and appreciated everything. When I shifted how I looked at my life, my life shifted. The situation didn't change, my perspective changed. When we look at things differently, things look different. I was no longer a woman who was not good enough, but an incredible woman who worked my way through four academic degrees, each one under some very trying circumstances. I was not that incompetent weakling that I thought. I was not less than others, or less valuable. I don't waver, I persevere. I needed to recognize these traits so I could unconditionally love and respect myself. I wasn't comfortable taking care of myself, it was much easier to care for others. But by loving and respecting myself I could treat others with respect. My fears and low self-esteem were the primary root cause of my unhappiness and unworthiness, and my feeling jealous of others who appeared to have everything. I have many tools that I use today to help me stay grounded, tools like walking, meditating, EFT, journaling, talking to a friend, whatever I need to do to stay in the day, and in the moment. I am happy and healthier than I ever was.

Guilt – another difficult *lemon* that takes our power away and gives others control. Staying in *guilt* does not solve the problem, it prolongs the problem. *Guilt* is enslavement. Unlike the *lemons* of *fear* and anxiety that were with me since childhood, *guilt* is something I adopted much later in life, mostly in regard to my children. Subjecting them to the barrage of screaming fights, dragging my little daughter out of bed in the cold of winter to search of her father, picking on them when I was angry at Danny, the list can go on and on. It was my daughter who would comfort me after one of our battles, even when she was only a toddler. As a two-year-old, my precious little girl would crawl on my lap and wrap her skinny self around me and tell me not to cry. Fifteen years later she did the same thing when Danny confessed to me about his affair with my girlfriend. In more recent years it was the long hours I worked, getting home too late and being too tired to cook a decent meal. My two oldest had jobs and were fairly independent, but I still had my youngest son who wasn't a child, but not quite an adult either, he was left to fend for himself. I tried to be both mother and father to him, but I was too exhausted, too angry, too tired. And that only made me feel more guilty. To compensate for my *guilt*, I wound up giving him permission to do things I ordinarily would not let my other children do, or I bought him whatever he wanted, if he wanted a $200 pair of sneakers, I bought them, even though I could not afford them. Giving in to his demands and buying him ridiculous things didn't help the situation. All it did was spoil him and pile on the *guilt* some more. Like everything else, I could not change the past and the wrong that I did.

Becoming aware of my feelings, thoughts, perceptions, actions and experiences was the first step in the direction of personal change. *Not everything that is faced can be changed, but nothing can change until it's faced.* And that is what I did. I faced my lemons. As my *self-awareness* developed, so did my *self-concept. Self-concept* is an understanding of who we are. I gradually recognized that my negative *self-concept* and low *self-esteem* kept me bound in a dysfunctional marriage. I accepted outlandish behavior and the more I accepted it the worse I viewed myself, the lower the self-esteem, the more negative my self-concept. It was a vicious circle. What is even more outrageous is believing that Danny chose me over the other women which boosted a false sense of self-esteem. The combination of *self-awareness* and a positive *self-concept* increased my *self-esteem*, which blossomed into *self-love. Self-love* may be the greatest and most important love that we can experience in our life, but learning to love ourselves is not as easy to achieve as the song states. *Self-love* starts with *self-esteem. Self-esteem* is an attitude of acceptance, approval and respect toward oneself, manifested by personal recognition of one's abilities and achievements. Esteem itself is to regard with respect. Self-respect is to recognize our good qualities as well as our faults with neutrality. Low self-esteem is when we believe we are less than others, less valuable.

I lived in that perception for a very long time. *Self-love* is taking care of ourselves first. And I have made that commitment. I exercise daily, walk as often as the weather allows, I even started to jog down my favorite path, I eat better, I get my hair done by a professional, I went to a dermatologist to have some tiny veins on my face removed that always bothered me, but in the past, I didn't think enough of myself to do anything about them. I laugh now. I feel good about myself. I'm genuinely happy. For us to be of any use to anyone else we need to take care of ourselves. If we fall apart, all who are around us fall apart too. Most of us are caregivers in one form or another. We care for others first, often putting ourselves last. By giving so much of ourselves to others it provides the perfect excuse not to take too much time for ourselves. Giving completely to others and not taking care of yourself is like trying to drive a car without refueling. Sadly, we rarely notice that we are depleted until we have run out of gas and we become ill. I am not suggesting that you stop caring for others and only focus on yourself. Being of service and giving back is an admirable asset. Showing kindness and caring for others is the key to obtaining a fulfilling life. But we cannot care for others if we do not care for ourselves first. This may sound confusing, especially if you've been taught that to love yourself or give to yourself, is a selfish act. *Self-love, self-respect* and *self-esteem* are not synonymous with selfishness. Just the opposite. When we generally like ourselves, treat ourselves with respect and tend to our own needs and wants, we are happy, healthy individuals and a pleasure to be around. Embodying *self-love* is one of the greatest examples we can set for our children, our loved ones, and for our friends. For me, *self-love* was a huge undertaking, but little by little I became happy with being who I am. I have grown to love my perfectly imperfect self.

In becoming true to myself I stopped blaming others. I no longer sat around waiting for the other person to fill my needs and make me happy. What a relief it was to discover that no one is responsible for my feelings, choices, problems, wants, needs or happiness, just as I wasn't responsible for their feelings, choices, problems, wants, needs or happiness. Responsibility, or rather self-responsibility, is being accountable for our own actions, decisions and behaviors and allowing others to be responsible for theirs. Today I choose to respond to life, not react to it. It is an incredibly empowering feeling to be in charge and responsible for my actions, thoughts, and feelings.

Perfectionism and people-pleasing are two more of my lemons. I had a powerful need to be perfect, to cover up all my imperfections. I thought if I was as perfect as possible, I would get my husband to love me, but no matter how much I tried, it never worked. He still got drunk, he still had affairs. Each degree I received was certainly a boost to my ego, especially when friends complimented me on my achievements, but it still wasn't perfect enough for me. I could pretend on the outside that I had it all together, but on the inside, I felt like a failure. I wasn't able to see my progress or how far I had come; I could only see how far I still had to go. I, like many other individuals, wanted to be thought of as a good person. I was afraid of rejection and constantly sought approval. I desperately needed others to like me. Because of this unhealthy need, I had a difficult time saying no, which of course meant I could not set any kind of *boundary*, not even with my children. In my irrational thinking, I had to be perfect to please others. There is nothing wrong with wanting to please other people, there is a sense of joy when we make someone happy. The problem arises when we say or do things that we don't want to say or do. All that does is brew resentments.

There is no doubt that I am a people pleaser. By nature, I am a giver, it's unfortunate that there are many takers out there. So, it was vital for me to set *boundaries*. The idea of a boundary, or setting *boundaries*, was completely new to me. It wasn't until I was in Al-Anon when I first heard the word. The behavior that I lived with, as outrageous as it might have been for someone else, was the norm for me, so how could I know what unacceptable behavior was? For most of my life, I let everyone walk all over me. I had no rules for myself. It's easy to understand *boundaries* in the physical, such as between two parcels of land. A boundary is something indicating a border or limit. Part of *self-love* is developing healthy *boundaries*. Learning how to stand up for myself and set some limits was a difficult task for me. I realized that a key element to developing healthy *boundaries* is assertiveness. Being assertive is not being aggressive, but establishing rules for myself, which I wanted others to respect. When I learned to set *boundaries* by taking care of myself, I stopped being the doormat, when I changed my behavior and nurtured myself and learned *No* was a complete sentence. I learned to take my power back.

Boundaries are necessary in every relationship and in every area of our lives, including a room or a designated area of our home that we can call our personal space. Setting *boundaries*, whether literally or figuratively, physically or emotionally, is no different than setting aside a section of a room as your own. Part of *self-love* is developing healthy *boundaries*. *Boundaries* are rules we establish for ourselves, which we want others to respect. I needed to apply this concept of a physical boundary to my own value system of what I determined as acceptable and not acceptable. Setting *boundaries* makes you feel safe and in control of what you can control. It was so uncomfortable to start to learn this skill, I call it a skill because it didn't come naturally for me at all. I had to learn it, and practice it before it would come easier. I realized that a key element to developing healthy *boundaries* is being assertive, not aggressive.

Along with setting *boundaries* comes the skill of *communicating*, expressing wants and needs with confidence and honesty. It was a skill that I needed to develop. As a child, my means of communicating was to cry and whine. As an adult, especially when I was married to Danny, I still resorted to whining and crying, but I also did a lot of complaining and blaming, without ever addressing an issue. Mostly, I said what I thought others wanted to hear. I did not know how to state what was on my mind or in my heart without hurting someone or facing a confrontation. Basically, I am a quiet and reserved individual. I hid behind people who were bold, fearless, and forthright and stayed quietly in the background while I let others speak for me. People are not mind readers, if I needed my needs met then I had to be the one to communicate them. What helped give me the courage to communicate my feelings was to keep what I said in the "I", i.e. *I am not happy; I am angry.* The "I" statement prevents people from being defensive. The "I" statements are strictly my feelings, my thoughts, they are neither right nor wrong. It took many years for me to develop sound communication skills without the fear of being laughed at, or rejected. I also needed to improve my listening skills. I am a compassionate and empathetic listener; I have the ability to see both sides of an issue and am able to step back from raw emotions so that I can think more clearly and act rather than react. And although I have always been a fairly attentive listener, maintaining eye contact, and not interrupting or trying to finish the other persons' sentence, I needed to listen in order to understand so I could respond without feelings of shame or placing blame or criticism. I have come to respect other people's opinions and beliefs and understand that we each have our own perspective and see things differently. Part of healthy *communication* is also taking responsibility for my own words and actions and owning up to my mistakes.

Communicating my thoughts, or feelings or setting healthy *boundaries*, or expecting someone to listen as I spoke, was a huge challenge for me. It was a skill that I needed to work diligently on. There is a wonderful motto that I live by, "say what you mean, mean what you say, and don't say it mean," which is a great help for me. I do my best to be impeccable and authentic with my word. Striving for excellence is a positive quality, however, striving for perfection is self-defeating.

When I began investigating who I was, the more self-aware I became. What I saw was this helpless *victim* I allowed myself to be. I let others control me and make decisions for me. As I continued on this journey of self-awareness, I became conscious of my feelings, thoughts, and perceptions. I learned what my triggers were, my level of frustration, what situations or events would bring on feelings of incompetency and inadequacy. I also learned what my beliefs and values are, what motivated me, and how I respond or react to a situation. It is said that 10% of your life experience is dependent on what happens to you and 90% is based on how you respond. This statement emphasizes the importance of how we respond, especially when faced with conflicts or problems. When I lost control, I gave my power away, when I went within, I stayed calm and empowered. I never saw myself as controlling because I thought I was meek and weak, but I was always trying to control the outcome, and the more I tried to control the more I lost my power. Control isn't about controlling someone else or changing the outcome, it is controlling my emotions. Life became much calmer when I shifted from control to connection.

DEPRESSION EXERCISE

Are you isolating?

_____

_____

Are you avoiding family or friends?

_____

Have you lost interest in favorite hobbies or pleasurable pursuits?

Do you feel tired? Listless? Have a hard time getting up in the morning?

Do you find yourself staying in bed all day over the weekends?

Do you have insomnia?

Are you maintaining personal hygiene?

Have you had a loss of appetite? Or overeating?

Weight gain? Weight loss?

Do you feel sad?

Do you find yourself crying?

Are you forgetting things?

What do you do to cope with depression?

PERFECTIONISM EXERCISE:

Do you consider yourself a perfectionist?

If so, in what area does being perfect mean the most to you?

How do you feel if you have not done something perfectly?

When you were a child, did your parents expect you to be perfect? Perfect grades? Perfect behavior?

Did your parents criticize imperfection?

When you find yourself berating a less-than-perfect performance, whether your own or someone else's, take a step back and see if you can view the situation as an observer. Are you able to acknowledge the positive parts of that performance or situation and not berate yourself for what you determine is your shortcoming?

Who do you want to be perfect for?

Overcoming perfectionism requires some degree of courage and a lot of honesty since it means accepting our imperfections and humanness. Think about the areas where you feel being perfect is of utmost importance and then decide what the advantages and disadvantages are of each. Such as the advantage of a perfect test score that lands you a job or promotion or the disadvantage of criticizing yourself or others because you or they do not meet your standard of perfection. Notice if you have a self-critical tendency or pattern of behavior. Do your best to substitute more realistic, reasonable thoughts for your habitually critical ones.

GRATITUDE EXERCISE:

What attitudes did you learn as a child? Did the members of your family help you to see the cup half-full or half-empty?

_____

_____

Without giving it too much thought, write down ten things in your life that you are grateful for.

_____

_____

_____

_____

_____

_____

_____

_____

_____

Keep an "Attitude of Gratitude" journal. Each evening take a few minutes before bedtime to write down at least five things that you are grateful for that day; it can be an event, circumstance, situation, activity, person, place or thing. By writing what it is you are grateful for, you will start to shift your negative behavior patterns. It will become a habit to focus on what you do have, rather than what you do not have, to see your abundance, instead of lack.

You can use statements such as:

The thing I liked most about_____

is_____.

Thank you for _____.

I appreciate it when you_____.

I am happy because _____.

I am grateful for_____.

SELF-LOVE EXERCISE:

What do you like about yourself?

_____

_____

What do you do to take care of yourself physically, mentally, emotionally?

_____

_____

When was the last time you had a visit with a doctor or the dentist for a checkup?

_____

Do you ever put yourself first?

What are the circumstances when you do put yourself first?

How do you respond when someone gives you a compliment? Are you able to answer with a simple thank you? Or do you feel the need to lessen your act of kindness, (it was no big deal) or go on about the dress not costing very much, (it was on sale, borrowed or old)?

Is there anything or anyone that you feel stops you from doing what you what to do?

How do you see your self-esteem?

What are some things you can do to nurture yourself?

Make a list of some of the things you enjoy, but deny yourself.

_____

_____

Make a commitment to yourself. Each day, for one month, do something special for yourself, at the end of the month write about how you feel.

_____

_____

Set some realistic goals if you need to lose or gain weight. Speak to professionals on how to improve your diet, or establish an exercise program designed for your body. You can begin nurturing yourself no matter what you may think about you. It doesn't take money to boost your self-esteem. It takes self-love.

THINGS I DID TO RAISE MY SELF-ESTEEM:

I accepted complete responsibility for myself, the way I thought, what I said and what I did.

I choose to direct my life in constructive channels (I entered into Doctorate Program.)

I refrained from criticizing myself.

I learned to set healthy boundaries.

I made a decision to accept my consequences for my own actions.

I disciplined my thoughts.

I had to purge myself of all blame, shame and guilt.

I refused to accept blame and shame from others.

I had to learn to be authentic to my own values.

I learned to stand up for my opinions.

I learned to financially support myself.

I learned to greet people with a smile.

I learned from my mistakes.

SELF-AWARENESS EXERCISE:

Who are you?

_____

_____

What do you think of yourself?

_____

_____

What makes you different from others?

_____

_____

How do you control your actions?

_____

_____

What values do you live by?

_____

_____

Are you aware of your thoughts?

_____

BOUNDARIES EXERCISE:

What boundaries are important to you?

_____

_____

Is anyone violating your boundaries?

_____

_____

Have you expressed your boundaries in a clear, concise and confident manner?

_____

_____

SELF-RESPONSIBILITY EXERCISE:

Do you feel you are responsible for your own actions?

_____

_____

Do you assume other people's responsibility?

_____

_____

Do you feel you are responsible for your own happiness?

_____

_____

Who do you feel you are responsible for?

_____

_____

Make a list of some situations that you either blamed someone else or felt they were the ones responsible. Can you identify what your part was?

_____

_____

Did you create the situation?

_____

_____

What were your thoughts?

_____

_____

What did you say? Or what could you have said?

_____

_____

Ask yourself, 'what can I do differently to get the results I want?'

_____

_____

There is no right or wrong, just let the pen flow. Once you have everything written down, see what your responsibility was. If you could do it over, what would you change in your behavior, beliefs and attitudes? You will be able to make wiser choices in the future once you take responsibility for your life.

COMMUNICATION EXERCISE:

Are you able to express what you are feeling or thinking?

_____

_____

Do you shut down the communication? When? Why?

_____

_____

How important is it to you to improve your communication skills?

_____

_____

What is your non-verbal communication? Does it need improvement?

_____

_____

Do you tell lies in order not to hurt another?

_____

_____

How do you best communicate? Verbally, written, or through actions?

_____

_____

Do you communicate better with some people? Why?

_____

_____

How do you react when someone misunderstands you? Do you become defensive? Angry? Withdraw? Impatient?

_____

_____

Are you assertive? Or are you aggressive?

_____

_____

Are you an attentive listener?

_____

_____

NOTES:

Release Lemons of:
Negative Beliefs

Add Ingredients of:
Positive Beliefs

Healing Practice:
EFT Tapping, Practicing Mindfulness, Self-Talk

Today's accomplishments were yesterday's impossibilities.
~Robert H. Schuller

You can complain because roses have thorns, or you can rejoice because thorns have roses. My *lemon* of *negative belief* limited my success and prevented me from feeling good about myself. Any habitual pattern of thinking is called a belief. Beliefs may be based on statements and comments we heard as a child from a parent, a teacher or someone of authority, or someone that we believed and trusted. When you hear critical, degrading comments long enough, we believe them. As I did. Living in a twenty-year dysfunctional marriage to a man who lied, had repeated affairs and criticized everything I did, led me to believe there was something wrong with me, why else would he cheat. I believed I was an unattractive, unintelligent, helpless individual not capable of making even the smallest decision. I believed I was unlovable. This affected my attitude, the way I felt, the way I acted, the way I looked and every decision I made. The beliefs became internal and they took my power away. The more I was emotionally battered the stronger my *negative beliefs* became until I believed that I would never succeed at anything. I was trapped in my own beliefs.

This toxic thinking spilled into every area of my life. I had one setback after another. What I didn't realize at the time was the setbacks were making me stronger. The more obstacles that were put in my path, the more I had to learn to go over them, under them, around them or through them to get to the other side. I had to learn to focus on the good. Focus on the positive side of the *negative beliefs*. It was becoming obvious how powerful my thoughts were. My thoughts shaped my experiences, they determined my attitude and my attitude determined how I treated myself, and how I treated myself let others know how they can treat me. When my thoughts were positive, I generated positivity, and when my thoughts were negative, I created negativity. My thoughts were subconscious and they were the rules I lived by. When I consciously chose to reprogram my thinking, I influenced and controlled my life from the inside out. When I changed my thinking habits, I changed my life. If I was unhappy with my life circumstances, I had to begin with changing my thinking process and self-talk.

As I started to change my thinking and the words I used, my life experiences started to change. I couldn't make a positive change in my life until I could identify my negative thinking patterns. Negative thinking held me back from being the person I was born to be. Both negative and positive thinking give the same power to a situation. I could literally talk myself into or out of a feeling, thought or belief. I couldn't help but to believe what I continually told myself. When I placed my focus on negative aspects, on what I lacked and did not have in my life, I only produced more of what I did not have or like. It's known as the law of attraction, what we attract by our thoughts, words and feelings, is what we will receive. If I wanted positive changes to occur and feel really good about myself, then I needed to change my mental story. I had choices, I could stay stuck in the feeling of lack and negativity and believe that I was incapable or I could shift my thoughts and focus on what I did have and see myself as an intelligent, beautiful being, capable of creating whatever I wanted.

As I began to observe my thoughts and the words I habitually used and changed the *negative beliefs* into positive uplifting truths, I had the potential to improve every area of my life. As I gradually shifted from a positive frame of mind the "stinking thinking" no longer felt comfortable. I came to believe and accept that I was capable of doing, being and having anything

I set my mind too. Thoughts are that powerful. I shifted my thinking to what I was grateful for, and when my attitude changed, I felt better and when I felt better, I could focus on what I could do to create a better atmosphere for myself. I also recognized the power of words and how a word could bring about a positive feeling or a negative one. The word *should* for instance, put demands on myself and took over my power. I should have done this; I should have done that. Should is a hard-punishing word. Changing should to *could* was kinder, it gave me back my power because it became my decision, my choice. *Can't* was another word that needed a quick exit from my vocabulary. Can't rendered me helpless. On the other hand, I can or I will, are uplifting confident words, loaded with empowerment. Changing from negative words to more positive gentle words helped me to change my feelings from not believing, to maybe it's possible, to feeling hopeful, to feeling better, to I believe.When my belief matched my desire, the outcome became possible. No matter how much I wanted something, like making more money and fulfilling my dream of helping other women, it was less likely of happening if I didn't believe it could. I learned that once I believed something, I could achieve it.

Self-esteem, self-love and faith are closely related to positive thinking, as is gratitude. When my self-esteem grew and I was able to see my own value and worth it was then possible for me to believe that I could use my experiences to help other women. To help myself think in a positive manner and open my mind to all possibilities I made a vision board. I used colorful pictures and empowering words from magazines, set goals and planned strategies of how to obtain them. Smaller short-term goals helped me attain the larger long-term ones, from organizing book shelves to completing my doctorate, to opening my own business, to writing a book on empowerment. Breaking my negative thinking habit was a challenge, but all I needed to do was see how far I had come and my spirits were lifted and positive thoughts took over. I still go through "stinking thinking" but it doesn't last long at all. The longer I stay focused and conscious of my thoughts, my words and feelings, the better I feel. I have even learned that when I make a mistake it is just a mistake; a mistake doesn't change who I am. It doesn't define me. The more I shifted my thoughts, beliefs, feelings and actions, the more empowered I became and the more I was in control of my life.

I learned to utilize the ABCDE model, when an experience would trigger negative thoughts, I used self-talk to work my thoughts from A (adverse event) to E (energized).

A = An adverse event occurs.

B = You immediately have some negative beliefs and thoughts about the adverse event.

C = You experience the consequences of having these thoughts and beliefs, including negative emotions.

D = You intentionally dispute your negative beliefs.

E =You feel energized when you successfully dispute your negative thoughts and realize that the situation is not as you initially believed.

I practiced this exercise every time I caught myself thinking negatively. When I made a conscious effort to reboot my negative thoughts things started to become hopeful. With time and effort, reframing beliefs, thoughts, and emotions became my regular way of thinking. When I made this part of my daily routine, it had great personal benefits.

NEGATIVE BELIEF EXERCISE:

List your limiting beliefs. Select one belief at a time.

Try to recall where and when you first heard this belief.

What beliefs came from your childhood?

Do you feel that your beliefs about yourself or your situation will help change your life?

Who do you believe you really are?

It has taken a lifetime for you to acquire these limiting *negative beliefs*. Be patient with yourself, reprogramming the old pattern of thinking is a moment-to-moment process. Each time you state or think one of your limiting beliefs immediately change it to a positive one.

YOUR POSITIVE STATEMENTS NEED TO CONTAIN THREE ESSENTIAL COMPONENTS:

1. Begin your statement with the word "I"
2. Followed by the word "am"
3. Then your positive description

REPLACING NEGATIVE BELIEFS WITH A POSITIVE STATEMENT.

Example:

I am helpless.............................I am powerful

I can't...................................I am able to achieve anything I want

I am not responsible....................I am responsible

I am a victim of events.................I am free to choose how I respond to my life events

I can't learn anything..................I am always learning new things

I can't change...........................I am capable of changing

POSITIVE THINKING EXERCISES FOR REPROGRAMMING THE THOUGHT PATTERNS:

How do you view your life? Do you see the cup half-empty or half-full?

_____

_____

Observe your language, what you say, how you say it.

Replace negative words with positive ones. Such as *I can't*, to *I can* or *I will.*

How can you change your negative thinking?

_____

_____

Practice Affirmations: affirmations are positive personal comments, which replace negative thoughts.

I am fat – I am a beautiful individual.

I am stupid – I am an incredibly intelligent woman.

I am not worthy of love – I am worthy of all of God's gifts, especially love.

I love all of me, my body, my mind and all of my feelings.

- Practice Verbalization: speak aloud to yourself in order to notice language patterns and change the negative language to positive outcomes.
- Practice Visualizations: which is mental imagery, 'picturing' what it is you want, visualizing every detail, including how you would feel. Emotional energy is imperative in obtaining what it is you want.
- Associate with positive people: being in the company

of positive-minded people is a wonderful source of support.

- Acting the part: behave 'as if' you already have successfully created what it is you want.

Every time a negative thought enters your mind you need to replace it with a positive thought, even if you don't feel it is true. You really do have a choice in how you think. You can give up and carry on reinforcing your old limiting beliefs or you can live your new empowering sentences and work on changing your beliefs.

The last step to this exercise is to write down three positive statements about yourself, they do not need to be true, just yet. It is what you would like to see yourself as. Use these new statements as if they already exist. These new *positive beliefs* will gradually create your new self-image.

NOTES:

Add Ingredients of:
Family and Friends, Life Purpose, Joy/Laughter, Humor

Healing Practice:
Meditation, Connecting with Nature, Reiki, Service, Law of Attraction

*"Do not go where the path may lead, go instead where there is no path
and leave a trail."*
~ Ralph Waldo Emerson

It is a scientific fact that *laughter* boosts the immune system, reduces the risk of heart disease, lowers high blood pressure and increases the will to live. A good sense of *humor* and the ability to laugh at stressful situations can mitigate the damaging effects of distressing emotions. *Laughter* helps us roll with the punches that inevitably come our way. *Laughter* is a natural life-saving gift for coping and for survival. *Laughter* is healing. *Laughter* is one of the easiest ways to free the mind from the constant flow of negative thoughts and find inner peace. *Laughter* is the best medicine. It is a universal language. It's a contagious emotion and natural diversion. It breaks down barriers and allows other people in. It is the shortest distance between two people, it can unite us, especially when we laugh together. Best of all, it is free, and it has no adverse effects! When in my deepest darkest moments, I wasn't in the mood to laugh, nor could I find any *humor* about my situation. Thankfully, I have many *friends* who not only lift me up but have me laughing, especially at ourselves. The weekend that Danny sent Joy and I to the Bahamas to get rid of me could have been spent crying or raging, but instead, Joy had me laughing the whole time, especially when she won money at the slot machine and dragged me back to our room, nearly peeing ourselves we laughed so hard. When I lost my job, I had more time to spend with my grandchildren who were two and three years old at the time. There is nothing that can get you laughing like listening to their little innocent conversations.

Without a doubt, my greatest gift of all has been my amazing *family* and an awesome circle of *friends*. Over the years I have had the good fortune to be surrounded by several close *friends*, without their unconditional love, endless support and genuine kindness I don't think I could have made it to where I am today. These incredible individuals carried me through a difficult journey and I am forever grateful to each of them. Each one is unique. Because of them, I was given stability, loyalty, faith, companionship, honesty, outrageous humor, confidence, validation, generosity, money, hugs, shoulders to cry on, strength, courage, creativity, and help with business decisions, real estate, financial assistance and completing my doctorate! There have been so many who have touched my life, some briefly, but all in an extraordinary way. And then there is my *family* from whom I have received absolute and unconditional love. A special note to my mother. She stood beside me through every crisis, allowed me the dignity to walk my own path, never judged me even when I judged myself. She was the first person I'd call when I was sad, angry, upset, in a rage, in grief, or in joy. It was her house that I went to everyday from work to hide from the ever-present reporters. She'd feed me, comfort me and help me through. Because of her, this book was written. Last, but certainly not least, are my three remarkable children, Rachelle, Dan and Tony, and my precious half-sister Seline, who are each a light in my heart and the loves of my life. They are my safe circle of support, they ground me and put me back on the path I need to be.

It's important for me to mention faith again. It was, and still is, my constant ingredient. When I didn't have money, I had my *faith*. After my car was repossessed, I went over a year without a vehicle of my own. I had no idea how I could get another car without money and poor credit. When I listed my goals for January, I wrote that I needed a good running car. Then I turned it over to God and my angels to handle the details without me trying to figure out how this could happen. Lo and behold, less than two weeks into the new year, my brother offered me a car that he had. It was in good shape, both inside and out. Years before when Carol and I were just starting out it was our faith that got us through, right from the beginning when we needed to raise $400 at our yard sale to purchase the puppets, and we made $400.93! That is *faith*. I have had many "gifts" of this nature over the years. At the same time that I had gained full custody of my half-sister, Seline, I was also at the end of my doctoral studies. After taking a year off to finish my academic work, I wasn't sure how I was going to support her. Once again, I turned it over to God and trusted it would work out, and it did. I was hired for a Director's position at a private child care facility. One of the best perks was free child care, which I used for five years! This was the perfect job for that point and time in my life, but once Seline started school the long distance to work and the amount of time on the road became a problem. I put my energy into looking for something closer and was again blessed with another wonderful position, this time as a director of a youth program working with adolescents, and was only half an hour from my home. Perfect! I loved being with this age group helping these teens learn a better way to live and encouraging them to continue their education. It was so rewarding witnessing the change in these teens, seeing many of them graduate high school though they never imagined possible, and making positive changes in their difficult young lives. But the job ended without warning when the grant that sponsored the program was not renewed. I was shocked, angry, and very sad to say goodbye to these kids and a program that I worked hard to develop. The end of this position wasn't my choice. I found myself in flux again, frustrated and in turmoil. I started scribbling thoughts on paper, just as I had before when creating my first book. The scribbles steadily increased, the more I wrote, the more I gained clarity that I needed to share my life experiences. Through the tragic events in my life, I found my *life purpose*, to help empower other women and give them a sense of hope. My pastors' comments became very clear to me. I needed the time off from work to just STOP and heal. My life experiences would instill hope in others.

Some people have a dream since childhood but never felt worthy enough to pursue. Others, including myself, never thought about a *life purpose*. I was too busy expending my energy to simply survive. But once I explored the journey of putting the pieces of my life together, identifying my *lemons* that were the crux of my unhappiness, and gradually adding new empowering *ingredients*, I was able to reflect on my *life purpose*. The more I gained an understanding of myself, the more I had to work worth. Self-knowledge is empowerment. When I feel strong and confident, I feel capable of inventing the life I want. As I began to feel empowered, I learned that I really could live a fulfilling life by creatively capitalizing on my talents, values and passions. Passion stimulates the energy that is the motivating force towards creating the life of our dreams.

My passion, for as long as I can remember was working with children. My first degree was in Early Childhood Education. I loved getting up in the morning and spending the day at the pre-school I worked at. Over the years my love for helping children evolved into co-founding a center of education for youth and their families on alcohol and drug addiction. The center served a two-fold purpose for me, it was a place where I could utilize my talents and it was also my refuge from my dysfunctional marriage and chaotic home life. The worse my marriage got, the more I pushed myself into my work and continuing with my education. Digging into my studies was my therapy. It was a way for me to block out the misery from sharing my life with a man who repeatedly lied and cheated. I don't like to admit this, but the end of my marriage was not my choice. The question that haunted me was how I got from a young hopeful bride to a woman struggling to stay sane. That one question began my journey of self-discovery. Scribbling my thoughts on paper, evolved to a book, and the gradual healing process began. The more I wrote, the more I discovered about myself. I didn't focus on the outcome, I knew it was more about the process and while I was absorbed in the process, my goal was achieved. I did it one step at a time. One day at a time. One thought. One word. One paragraph. One chapter. Out of a tragic event, I discovered my passion and *life purpose*, to help empower other women. Sometimes I achieve this through a casual conversation, other times by an afternoon workshop, or maybe one woman reads my book and finds the courage to change her life.

Recently, my friend Annie and I started a social network for women, *"100 Days of I & A – Inspiration and Accountability"*. Our mission is to guide and inspire women to make a commitment, to be accountable and to inspire other women to be the best version of themselves. The 100-day commitment encourages women to take care of themselves in whatever way they need on that particular day, maybe it's cardio, weight training, a slow gentle yoga session, or a walk-in nature or meditation, thereby, caring for our body, our mind and our soul. In just a few short weeks the number of women grew to more than we ever imagined, women of all ages and all body sizes and shapes and all walks of life. Remember you and you alone are the chef of your own life; only you can add the empowering ingredients to become the best version of yourself. The results will depend on how much you want to change your defeating behavior patterns and whether you desire a small piece of that delicious lemon meringue or the entire pie. Take it from me – go for the whole thing – you are worth it! The only thing standing between you and feeling empowered is your commitment to yourself. So, take the risk, do the work and your life will change.

HUMOR EXERCISE:

- Practice smiling. A smile is the beginning of laughter. Smile at strangers you pass on the street. Smile at the waitress, the gas station attendant, the cashier, the mailman, even if you know he is delivering a stack of bills.
- Refer to your gratitude list. The simple act of gratitude for the good things in your life will help keep those negative thoughts at bay that are a barrier to humor and laughter.
- Seek out laughter. It takes added effort to find humor when we're feeling sad, grumpy, overwhelmed, or negative. Keep some funny movies or a book of jokes handy in times of need. They may not get you on the floor roaring, but it might lift your spirits enough to get through a difficult time.
- Pal around with people who have a good sense of humor. Their lightheartedness is contagious. Laughs and smiles are enjoyed best when shared with others.

FAMILY/FRIEND EXERCISE:

Do you have a relationship with both parents? Mother? Father?

_____

_____

Are your parents divorced? Deceased?

_____

_____

Were you raised by a stepparent? Another relative? If so, what is your relationship with that person?

_____

_____

Do you have siblings? If so, what is your relationship with them?

_____

_____

Do you have close friends?

_____

_____

What do you do for enjoyment?

_____

_____

Do you prefer the company of others? Or to be alone?

_____

_____

Would you like to have more or less of a social life?

_____

_____

LIFE PURPOSE EXERCISE:

If money weren't an issue, what would you do?

_____

What are your hobbies?

_____

_____

What are your talents and abilities?

_____

_____

Do you remember what you wanted to be as a child?

_____

_____

Did you like to draw? Play teacher? Nurse?

_____

_____

Did you love animals? Sports? Helping in the kitchen?

_____

_____

What brings you joy and happiness? Travel? Sewing? Decorating? Puttering in the garden? Tinkering with mechanical things? Writing?

_____

_____

Do you like to probe and investigate? Work with numbers?

_____

_____

Do you like to be in the center of attention? Do you prefer working alone?

_____

_____

What kind of people do you like to be around?

_____

_____

If you had your family's support, what would you choose to do?

_____

_____

Do you have a vision? A goal? An idea?

_____

_____

How do you see your life one year from now? Two? Five?

_____

_____

What would your life mission statement be?

_____

_____

Think about what you love and what it might take to get you there. Start with creating a vision board. Use large poster paper or a corkboard, sift through magazines and the Internet and collect pictures. Tack a picture of yourself on the board, put your photo standing in front of wherever it is you want to go, accepting your degree, or sitting in your new car. Be creative! If you don't know what you want, paste affirmations and inspirational words that help you feel good, such as, "I am open and receptive to new ideas", "happiness is...", "Joy", "Attitude of Gratitude", and so on. Use bright colorful paper. Begin to look around you, look at people wherever you go, get ideas. Look at yourself, smile. See yourself the way you want to be, envision doing what you want to do. Place your vision board where you can see it every day. Look at it every morning and evening just before bed. Make it bright, active and inspiring. Don't forget to put a date on it. Be true to yourself and you will see your vision come to life, you will live the life you were born to live. When you discover your life purpose, your life becomes very meaningful. It doesn't have to take a tragedy like the one I experienced for you to discover your life purpose. If I can move from a place of despair to living my dream - you can too.

You did it! You peeled your lemons, you've cleared the clutter, weeded out the negative beliefs and discovered some astounding positive qualities that were buried beneath layers of old myths. You're ready, willing and confident to whip up the most amazing batter of incredible ingredients and live an empowering joyful life.

I wish you well on your exciting journey of self-love, self-awareness and *empowerment!*

As Alexander the Great said,
"There is nothing impossible to him who will try."

"Nothing is impossible. The word itself says *"I'm Possible."*
Audrey Hepburn

NOTES:

ACKNOWLEDGMENTS

I have been blessed with an amazing family and an awesome circle of friends, without their gentle embrace I doubt if I could have made it to where I am today. You have all made a difficult journey easier, although "thank you" is not adequate enough to describe how much each of them means to me.

The love I have for my children Rachelle, Danny, and Tony cannot be expressed in a few printed words, against the odds they blossomed into fine adults. And to my half-sister, Seline, it is my honor to be your mother. I am eternally grateful to each of them and proud beyond description, they are the loves of my life.

I am so blessed to have four beautiful grandchildren, who are a constant joy and light up my life like I never imagined!

A very, very special thanks to my younger wiser brother, Roger Shore, for all our heart-to-heart talks and for being such a wonderful role model to my sons. You have always been my tower of strength. Words cannot measure my love.

My beautiful angel, my niece Candice, for sending me hundreds of heart rocks when I needed them the most. I do believe in miracles.

Joy Barnett- my dear sister of choice and childhood friend- I am forever grateful for her outrageous humor and ability to make me laugh when I wanted to cry. I love you, my friend.

Thanks to the senior Yaya's, LeLonni Campbell, for her wise astrological guidance; Charyl Ozkaya for her voice and gentle manner for the many EFT, breathing, and Reiki sessions, her voice alone is calming; and Phoenix Redhawk for bringing magic into my life.

Dottie Vocht-Mato for taking the time out of your busy life to read my manuscript and for providing me with your constructive suggestions.

A special thanks to Anne Moston for inspiring me to take this book out from under my bed and share my experience, strength and hope with other women. I am so excited for our new journey!

A heartfelt thanks to Red Penguin Books for helping me transform my project into a reality.

RESOURCES

Dr. Tamara Pelosi

Recipe to Empower Your Life

Workshops*Coaching*Public Speaking

www.drtamarapelosi.com

Drtamarapelosi@gmail.com

Dr. Tamara Pelosi & Anne Moston

Life Coaching for Woman's Wellness

Mind* Body* Soul*

www.100daysofianda.com

Charyl Ozkaya - Inner Healing Arts

Reiki Sessions * EFT * Breathwork * Meditation

Office/cell: 516-532-7633

www.innerhealingarts.com

Josephine Ghiringhelli

Psychic Medium * Intuitive Counselor * Public Speaker

www.josephineg.com

631-698-4089

LeLonni Campbell

Master Astrologer for over 30 years

lonniastrology@optimum.net

631-375-2166

Phoenix Redhawk

Reiki Master Teacher * Clinical Hypnotherapist *

Holistic Practitioner

www.sacredfeatherhealingarts.com

1sacredfeatherhealingarts@gmail.com

ABOUT THE AUTHOR

Tamara Pelosi earned her Doctorate in Education in 2007, but it was the 'school of life' that was her principal teacher. *Recipe to Empower Your Life* was born out of her own experience and motivated her to come forward and reveal her personal life for the sole purpose of helping other women.

Dr. Pelosi co-founded "Sunshine Prevention Center", a youth and family center dedicate to the needs of the community. Throughout the years, Tamara has created numerous parenting workshops, developed programs specifically for teachers, and facilitates support groups that help empower women to gain their independence.

Dr. Pelosi has been the recipient of numerous awards attesting to her charitable character: the <u>Suffolk Domestic Violence</u>

Coalition for her "courage"; the Women on a Mission Organization for her 'mission work with women and children'; Tamara was inducted into the Long Island Volunteers Hall of Fame; 'The Women of the Year' award for creating a variety of programs that serviced the youth and family of the local community; and the "Suffolk County Volunteer Award" for outstanding service to the youth of Suffolk County, New York.

In 2015 Dr. Pelosi wrote and self- published "Recipe for Creating a Peaceful Classroom", in addition, to creating a comprehensive Early Childhood teacher training program.

Dr. Pelosi is the Co-owner of "*100 Days of I & A – Inspiration and Accountability*". The mission of this social network is to guide and inspire women to make a commitment, to be accountable and to inspire other women to be the best version of their self physically, mentally and spiritually.